MASTERS AT WORK

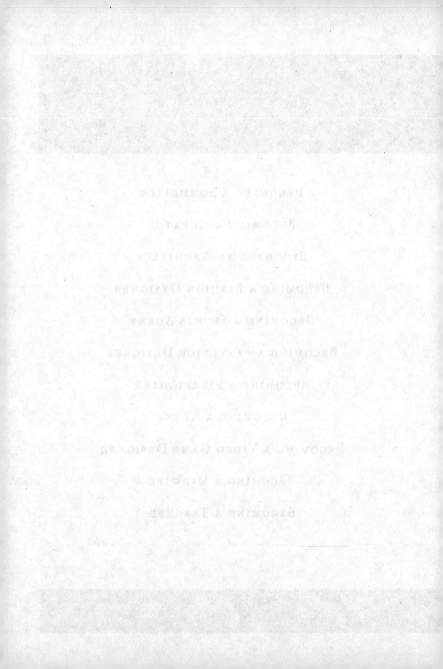

MASTERS AT WORK

BECOMING A CRIME SCENE INVESTIGATOR

JACQUELINE

DETWILER-GEORGE

SIMON & SCHUSTER PAPERBACKS

New York   London   Toronto   Sydney   New Delhi

YEARS

SIMON &
SCHUSTER
PAPERBACKS

An Imprint of Simon & Schuster, LLC
1230 Avenue of the Americas
New York, NY 10020

First Simon & Schuster trade paperback edition January 2024

SIMON & SCHUSTER PAPERBACKS and colophon are registered
trademarks of Simon & Schuster, LLC

Simon & Schuster: Celebrating 100 Years of Publishing in 2024

For information about special discounts for bulk purchases, please contact Simon &
Schuster Special Sales at 1-866-506-1949 or business@simonandschuster.com.

The Simon & Schuster Speakers Bureau can bring authors to your live event. For
more information or to book an event, contact the Simon & Schuster Speakers
Bureau at 1-866-248-3049 or visit our website at www.simonspeakers.com.

Illustrations by Donna Mehalko

Manufactured in the United States of America

10 9 8 7 6 5 4 3 2 1

Library of Congress Cataloging-in-Publication Data has been applied for.

ISBN 978-1-9821-3989-6
ISBN 978-1-6680-4971-6 (pbk)
ISBN 978-1-9821-3992-6 (ebook)

For those whom justice did not serve.

CONTENTS

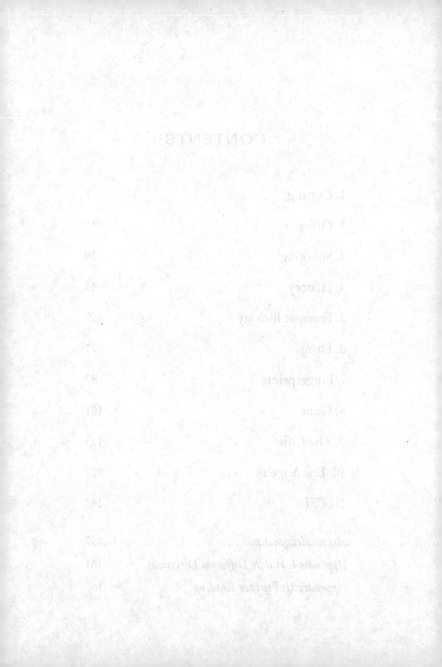

Becoming a
Crime Scene Investigator

———

1

CUTTING

Behind the convenience store, in full view of a broken surveillance camera, a camping chair and a blood-stained blanket sit abandoned in the urban blight. A pool of blood cools into gel on the sidewalk, separated from the rest of civilization by two fluttering lines of yellow crime scene tape. Past the police line, brick apartments squat on and on and on.

A passerby peeks over the tape. "He got him three times in the back and once in the chest!" he shouts.

But that is almost certainly not what happened.

What did happen behind this convenience store is, at this moment and legally speaking, a mystery. According to the dispatch call, it was a "cutting," a police department term for what would colloquially be called a stabbing. Jill, a blunt, raspy-voiced officer for the Baltimore Police Department, arrived soon after it happened. She chased the suspect across the street, where she detained him. Then she walked back to the scene, hunting for witnesses. She found only one.

Back at headquarters, crime laboratory technician Erika Harden was just beginning her ten-hour shift. The call came through around five p.m., while she was prepping her equipment. Over the radio, Harden announced that she was "10-8," the code for in-service, then took the elevator down to the bay, a cavernous garage that acts as a staging area for the crime lab. She loaded her gear into a black, all-wheel-drive, midsize SUV marked FORENSICS, and headed into the literal sunset.

Over the millennia since the Cuneiform laws first codified rules of behavior for ancient civilizations in the Middle East, millions of people have been employed in an attempt to enforce them: Roman quaestors and Chinese prefects and Islamic *muhtasibs*; international tribunals and police departments equipped with military-style weaponry. Erika Harden represents the slickest, most postmodern moment in this historical procession. She is a professional crime solver who uses cutting-edge science to determine who is responsible for transgressions, so wrongdoers can be brought to justice and prevented from causing further harm. Using nothing but physical tools and logic, she travels backward through time, re-creating a crime in as much detail as a courtroom can stand.

This job has many names: crime scene investigator, evidence technician, forensic investigator, crime scene technician, crime scene analyst, and crime scene examiner among them. Technically, Harden is a Crime Laboratory Technician II, a title confusing enough that it has misled people into thinking it was a laboratory job. A more illustrative title is "criminalist." Like a numismatist is a student and collector of coins, a criminalist is a student of criminalistics, a person who collects evidence in order to understand a crime in as much detail as possible. A criminalist should not be confused with a criminologist, which is a person who attempts to explain social deviance on a grand scale by plumbing the depths of psychology, policy, and punishment. A criminalist doesn't worry about the *why* of a crime. She deals in more prosaic questions: When? How? And most important, who?

ERIKA IS TWENTY-SEVEN, BUT appears younger, with kohl-rimmed eyes, plastic-gauged earrings, and a silver nose ring. She looks more like the lead singer in a punk band than a crime lab technician, which she has been for three years, ever since graduating from Stevenson University in Owings Mills, Maryland, with her master's degree in forensic science. She works ten hours a night, four nights a week, which sounds onerous but isn't really. The traffic is better at night than it is during the day, and she's used to late hours. In between school and starting at Baltimore PD, Harden worked shifts at a local bar.

Like many of her generation, Harden discovered crime scene investigation through the CBS show *CSI*, which catapulted the profession to fame after it premiered on October 6, 2000. Although it's difficult to imagine after sixteen seasons and an unending series of sequels, spin-offs, and imitators, the general public knew next to nothing about criminalistics before *CSI*. For most of the profession's history, crime scene investigators toiled behind-the-scenes in obscurity. People used to just fall into the job through a well-timed classified ad, the military, or friends and family who worked in law enforcement. Then came the show, which crime scene investigators in the younger age ranges almost universally claim as their first exposure to the career. For all its cheesy one-liners, *CSI* introduced the country to a job that rode the balance between law enforcement and hard science, where a smart nerd who lacked squeamishness could serve justice just as well as a hard-boiled detective in a fedora. It was *Sherlock Holmes* with Luminol. *Scooby-Doo* with liquid chromatography mass spectrometry.

Was that even a real job?

It was. And Erika was lucky enough to have an aunt who could tell her all about it. Harden's aunt, Mary-Pat Whiteley, was a veteran crime scene investigator in the original mold. She started off as a fingerprint tech for the FBI, then transitioned into the lone crime scene investigator for Annapolis City, Maryland. Over Thanksgiving dinners, Harden and her aunt would discuss the intimate details of crime scene investigation until the rest of the family asked them to please shut up because they were grossing everyone out. Harden became the first person in her family to earn a college degree, then stayed on for a five-year bachelor's-to-master's option, becoming the first person in her family to earn a master's degree. And here we are.

If you saw Erika Harden working in the street, like she is now, you might mistake her for a police officer. She wears black tactical pants and a long-sleeved baselayer under a black bulletproof vest marked FORENSICS. She used to wear her hair in a ponytail, but switched to a pair of dark braids twisted into a bun after she almost dragged the ponytail's tip through some suspected blood. On her belt: a flashlight, pepper spray, keys, and a radio. No sidearm. Harden is a civilian.

Harden whips out a tablet and opens an app called Crime-Pad. She creates a new case, followed by a new scene, and the app automatically records the date and time. This scene is fairly straightforward: only one person has been injured; the suspect is in custody; there aren't weapons lying around; and the combatants didn't run for five blocks and leave haphazard trails of evidence all down the street. All Harden has to do is take notes and photos, collect evidence for analysis, and be on her way.

A tablet app for crime scene investigators may not sound as exciting as the James Bond–worthy lab gadgets featured on crime shows (we'll get to those), but CrimePad has been a monumental advance over the technology CSIs previously used to describe scenes, which amounted to scribbling observations in spiral-bound notebooks. CrimePad organizes observations, evidence, and sketches through a series of drop-down menus and customizable screens that serve as guidelines for documentation. It creates an electronic record that assists with future reconstructions, such as for cases that don't come to court for years. Understandably, some 250 police agencies across the country have adopted the app since it launched in 2014.

Now for the cool stuff. To collect physical evidence, Harden uses a personalized kit containing her camera, external flash, batteries, measuring devices, and envelopes. Disposable scalpels and box cutters for scraping up paint or cutting carpet. Tweezers for grabbing anything tiny. In case of an especially messy scene, she's got personal protection equipment: gloves, hard hat, fire boots, and coveralls. There are lift cards, brushes, powder, and tapes for collecting fingerprints. Swabs for blood and DNA.

There's more in the trunk: plastic bins loaded with paper sacks; red plastic biohazard bags; weighted and numbered yellow triangles to mark the positions of physical items on the ground; a sharps container. An arson kit contains metal paint cans inside which investigators can seal burned or fuming evidence. Every car contains a ladder, a tripod, a safety kit, and a metal detector.

For the sake of speed and efficiency, Harden doesn't get to use the department's coolest tools, such as the Leica C10 3D laser scanner, which creates a 360-degree, high-resolution image of a crime scene in minutes, except in the most serious situations: shootings that involve police, mass casualties, national news-type events. But the crime lab is always on the lookout for spy-caliber gadgets that they hope the department will swing enough budget to purchase. Recently they got a little DeWalt camera that can peek into a hole in a wall to search for projectiles. "It has a magnet that will pull it out for you," Harden says.

It's the time of the evening photographers call the magic hour, when the waning light makes headshots, wedding photos, and art prints come out color-true and crisp. Harden adds a photo element to her scene in CrimePad to note that she's taking pictures and pulls out her department-assigned

Nikon D7200 digital camera. She takes a long-range photo from the nearest large intersection, where a street sign and the convenience store's marquee can establish an address. She steps closer for midrange shots, squats for the close-ups.

Photography is such a critical part of crime scene investigation that it morphs into a hobby for many who do the job. In addition to fulfilling required compositions—long-range, midrange, and a close-up for every major detail—crime scene investigators need to take photos that are high resolution, focused on the correct items, and free of blur. Most investigators operate their cameras at least somewhat manually, adjusting the lighting, aperture, shutter speed, and ISO setting as the situation requires. So far, Harden hasn't gone crazy with photography, but she knows techs who do it on the side for income or fun. There's even a photography competition at the annual meeting of the International Association for Identification (IAI), a major trade group for crime scene investigators: only some of the photos are of dead people.

Harden opens an evidence element in CrimePad and types in a description of the bloody blanket lying near the scene of the cutting, which she collects wearing nitrile gloves and places into a paper bag. She would never store suspected blood in plastic, because one of the cardinal rules of crime scene investigation is that plastic can encourage the growth of bacteria that degrade DNA, rendering it unusable for analysis. This is the science part of forensic science—knowing *how* to collect evidence so that it can be analyzed and deployed in court is as important as knowing *what* to grab at a scene. Technically you could send anyone to recover evidence—a beat cop, an untrained civilian, the detective working a case—but this specialized procedural knowledge is why a trained technician will do the best job. A criminalist is, at her most fundamental level, careful. Her carefulness creates order, and order creates answers.

Normally, Harden would next drive over to one of Baltimore's ten or so hospitals to photograph the cutting victim's injuries, creating a second scene for the same case in her CrimePad app. Tonight she won't have to. Another technician on the night shift happens to be working his own call at the appropriate hospital and has offered to take Harden's photos in her stead. The techs do this for one another constantly. In a job requiring long shifts, constant focus, and inhuman flexibility, you never know when a small favor will allow you to trade an hour of overtime for an hour of much-needed sleep.

Harden takes off for headquarters just as the fire department arrives to hose off the remainder of the blood. The restoration of individual homes or businesses after a crime is the responsibility of the owners, and private crime scene cleanup organizations offer intensive decontamination, odor removal, and cleanup services for a fee. On public property, such as this sidewalk, the fire department usually handles it themselves.

"That wasn't as exciting of a scene as I thought it would be," says Becca Jackson, who is in her first year as the night shift's assistant supervisor and who has offered to drive an annoying journalist (me) around all night to watch the team work. I have never seen so much blood outside of a donation bag and make a soft *oh yes, very boring indeed* type sound while continuing to be surprised that police departments allow people to go on ride-alongs at all. Jackson continues, with resignation and dark amusement: "There will be more tonight."

If that seems cold, it is only because psychological distancing is part of the job. The eight investigators on Harden's ten-hour shift handle an average of fifteen to twenty scenes a night, collecting clues in shades from mildly unpleasant to nauseating. You can come across anything in this profession: a battered woman, a body crawling with bugs, a child pornography server. It is, perhaps, the best way to regularly come into contact with horrors that only appear to the rest of us when some awful, inconceivable event whisks away the curtain of ordinary life. As Jackson puts it: "If *we* have to come out, it's not a good day."

Thankfully, the average person rarely encounters crime scene investigators, but they are out there all the time, performing an essential service. The job sits at the intersection of forensic science and law enforcement, supporting the broader ecosystem of police work. Crime scene investigators provide intelligence that guides investigators, prosecutors, and juries on their way to confer justice. It is a job both immensely complex and inherently simple, the conceptual equivalent of the law's personal magnifying glass.

Most of the people you'll encounter in this book work for the Baltimore City Police Department, a team of professionals I shadowed, rode along with, and interviewed in the fall and winter of 2019–2020. Scattered throughout these pages are other experts I met or talked to along the way, at other departments, at industry conferences, and at forensics schools, as a necessary counterpoint. Although accurate numbers are difficult to track, the Bureau of Labor Statistics says there were 17,200 "forensic science technicians" as of 2019, and these workers are scattered across state and county labs, police departments, and private offices all over the country. Everywhere this job is practiced, it is practiced a little bit differently. Everywhere, it can be smelly, dangerous, and physically and emotionally punishing.

But it has its moments. At a stoplight on the way back to headquarters, a group of enterprising young black men is washing car windshields for tips. A boy who can't be more than sixteen approaches Jackson's driver's-side window and uses his squeegee to draw a heart on it in soap. You don't need me to tell you that cops are not always beloved in a city like Baltimore, a city with a deep history of racial injustice and police brutality, where the 2015 death of Freddie Gray in police custody incited days of protests and riots that presaged the national Black Lives Matter demonstrations of 2020. But the forensics vans don't make people angry. They inspire the kind of respect people have for the fire department. Jackson and Harden wield no guns, no handcuffs, no citation forms. They carry iPads, and fingerprint kits, and really cool cameras.

They don't come to punish; they come to solve. What is there to dislike about that?

2

OFFICE

The crime scene office at headquarters is a firehouse juxtaposed on top of an open-plan cubicle farm. The women, and it is overwhelmingly women, with seven female investigators and managers on tonight's shift to just three males, sprawl in black office chairs, waiting to get called out to service. It's all very *Ghostbusters* until you take in the walls (bland) and the carpet (abominable). Partitions between computers are decorated with the same collages of personal mementos, goofy calendars, and knickknacks you'd find in any white-collar office. Everyone in this room could be on the clock for tax preparation services. Only they're all wearing body armor.

CSI, *NCIS*, and even the various Sherlock Holmes adaptations make it seem as if crime scene investigators are omnipotent vigilantes who solve parades of horrors, night after night, in labs so kitted out they'd impress NASA. But that is not exactly it. There are reports to file. Boring tasks you have to perform over and over again. The perils can be the same as those in any other large, bureaucratic apparatus: limited resources, protocols, drudgery. You can have a smarter idea and still have to do as you're told.

Another way crime scene investigation differs from the way it is depicted on television is that, even in Baltimore, which suffers an abnormally high number of homicides, real calls rarely involve murder. Toward the end of 2019, the rate of murders handled by Baltimore's crime lab was about .027 percent, or 300 out of 10,911 total calls. The crime lab here goes out for all sorts of things—burglaries, assaults, shootings, cuttings, rape and sex offenses, arsons, carjackings, and questionable deaths. You never know what you're going to get, although around here burglary or assault is usually a good bet.

Which crimes warrant the services of the crime scene team and which do not? That's a good question, to which there is no national answer. If a national organization were to set an official standard, someone would have to ensure enough funding to carry it out across the country's approximately eighteen thousand law enforcement agencies, and that ain't happening. There are guidelines, of course, but in practice each department sets its own low bar, based on resources, crime volume, and how outraged a community would be if no one bothered to look too deeply into a particular situation. A burglary in a wealthy suburb, for example, might get the same treatment as a murder in South Chicago. Like almost everything having to do with law enforcement, responses are a patchwork: jurisdictions establish their own protocols, their training programs, and their definitions of crimes worthy of science.

While crime scene investigators can and do work scenes alone (this is why both Harden and Jackson carry pepper spray), they also do not perform all of the functions they are depicted handling on TV. Interviewing suspects, for example, is the purview of detectives (or patrol officers), although in some jurisdictions multiple jobs are rolled into one. In very small agencies, there may be no assigned CSIs at all, and sworn officers handle all the work themselves.

Crime scene investigators would also be unlikely to conduct an autopsy, analyze teeth, calculate time of death based on the life spans of flesh-eating bugs, or make pronouncements about age or sex from found bones. These activities are left to other experts within the larger world of forensic science, such as coroners or medical examiners, forensic dentists, forensic entomologists (insect experts), and forensic anthropologists.

What crime scene investigators *do* is collect and/or analyze evidence, usually with some degree of autonomy as to what, where, and how. Crime scene investigators have to comply with fourth amendment rights barring unlawful search and seizure, but within those bounds they are free to snoop as they wish. A crime scene investigator can choose, for example, which method of fingerprint collection would best suit a particular scene; she can choose what to photograph, with what lighting and from which angle. What an investigator takes and what she leaves is her decision, and that decision can have serious legal consequences.

Michael Lee, a sergeant and firearms examiner with the Michigan State Police, expressed this awesome responsibility poignantly at the 2019 meeting of the International Association for Identification in Reno, Nevada. He described a case he'd worked, back in 2014, in which a man had been discovered shot in the chest in his home. And what a home: it was the filthiest place Lee had seen in sixteen years of policework. The basement was a swamp. On the main floor, mice scurried with impunity through mounds of clothes and dog excrement. The dead man lay on a bed carpeted in a layer of dead skin so thick—Lee sounds ill just talking about it—it looked like sand.

The dead man's wife insisted that what had happened had been a suicide. But as investigators sifted through this grim scene, they found no guns. Without a weapon, it was difficult to believe the man had shot himself. What would he have shot himself *with*?

It took ten hours of searching to process the house. Investigators had to comb through a mountain of junk: the man had worked in a machine shop and pieces of unfinished metal floated through the flooded basement and lay scattered all over the main floor. The day heated up quickly, and the rooms became stuffy. As the investigators explored, they grew hungry, tired, nauseated. Eventually, they departed believing that they'd found everything they were going to find. The house contained no guns. It seemed possible they were looking at a murder.

But the detectives weren't sure. The next day, they returned to re-interview the dead man's wife. When they arrived, several pieces of metal, including a rod, a brass fitting, and a hollow cylinder, sat on a table. *I've never seen these before*, the wife told the detectives. *They seem out of place to me.*

One of the detectives brought the pieces back to the

firearms lab, where Lee saw that they could function as a rudimentary barrel, chamber, firing pin, and hammer. He examined one piece, the solid rod that had acted as a firing pin, under a microscope. Markings on it matched those on a cartridge they'd found inside a metal piece on the floor. Together, the pieces operated as a home-made gun, sometimes called a zip gun. The crime scene investigators—expecting to find something more in line with the common conception of a firearm—had missed it among all the random junk.

"You've got to give credit where credit's due," Lee says of the detectives' decision to return to the house. Sometimes the pitcher strikes out the batters, and sometimes the play gets all the way to the shortstop.

NOT TO BELABOR THE "it's different everywhere" point, but this job really is different in every place it's practiced. Large city and county police and sheriff's departments often have their own compartmentalized, in-house crime labs. Other law enforcement agencies collect evidence on their own and then send all or part of it to regional or state labs for processing. In some jurisdictions, such as Houston, an independent forensic science center sends its own crime scene investigators to work scenes alongside police.

In Baltimore, what a layperson might call "the crime lab" operates out of two parallel divisions. There's the forensic laboratory section, which processes evidence such as DNA, firearms, drugs, and fingerprints in-house, and then there's the crime scene unit, also called the "mobile unit," which travels to scenes to collect stuff. The mobile unit, a dedicated evidence recovery team, operates out of this office. When a call for a technician's unit number comes through dispatch, she loads up, heads out, and picks up whichever goods she—through much training—deems necessary to solving the crime. She doesn't manipulate or analyze anything once it comes in. She simply drops off her haul at evidence control and heads back here to wait for the next call.

There are benefits to compartmentalizing the work this way, both departmentally and personally. Departmentally, repeating the same tasks over and over again, rather than only attending an active crime scene once every few months or so, makes technicians smarter and faster. You know what to grab, where to search, and which camera filters can best illuminate what you're looking at. You develop tricks such as using a violet light source to illuminate old or subdermal bruises on a domestic violence victim. Erika Harden always makes sure to check for evidence under the seats in vehicles, under the beds in houses, and behind doors.

Interpersonally, processing scene after scene makes a night of work something like a military deployment. Adrenaline, carnage, and weird hours have made the women on Baltimore's mobile unit shifts as close as sports teams. Behind Becca Jackson's computer are photos of her and a few of the other night shift technicians hanging out in swimsuits at one of their family's beach houses in Cape May, New Jersey. They look like they're having fun, probably joking about something manifestly awful they saw at work that they can't talk about to anyone else. "It's like a second family," Jackson says.

Some of the bonding can be attributed to youth: many of the night shift technicians are in their twenties, pre-family, and still on the hunt for their social networks. The average age of Baltimore's crime scene teams is thirty-two, with techs as young as twenty-five and as old as their sixties. They are well-educated, the majority with undergraduate degrees in hard science. About half have master's degrees. They appear to come in two varieties: serious, focused public servants who lean into the job's responsibilities to maintain internal calm; and high-spirited optimists who forestall cynicism with deadpan senses of humor.

Here's an example: when we arrive back at the office, Jackson offers me my own bulletproof vest for the next call, in case it's something more dangerous than a cutting. She explains that all they have left among the spares are bulky blue vests you wear over your clothes, not the sleek black undershirt-style she and Harden are wearing. Walking by, Harden compares any and all bulletproof vests to anxiety protection devices for dogs. "I call it my thunder shirt," she says. Type 1. Type 2.

Blond, straight-backed and square-shouldered, Becca Jackson cuts the competent figure of a pilot. She is capable, measured, unflappable. Maybe it's a management thing: since being promoted to assistant supervisor last year, most of Jackson's evenings involve approving reports with the shift supervisor—her immediate boss, Rodney Montgomery—ensuring all the notes taken in the field are written as clearly and understandably as possible for their eventual day in court.

Otherwise, Jackson is very similar to Harden: She always fared well in science classes and got her first ideas about the career by watching *CSI* with her mom. She also had family members who worked in the world of law enforcement. She and Harden are even dressed the same, down to the double braid and bun. "Becca copied me, don't let her tell you different," Harden says.

In pursuit of her dream career, Jackson attended West Virginia University, the only school in the country to offer bachelor's, master's, and doctoral degrees in forensic science. The program is split into three tracks: biology, chemistry, and examiner, with each track funneling students toward a different type of forensic career. Biology track students usually go on to work as DNA analysts or pathology assistants. Chemistry track students become drug lab chemists, arson investigators, toxicologists, or trace evidence analysts. Jackson was examiner track, which prepares students for careers as crime scene analysts, fingerprint examiners, firearms examiners, or law enforcement.

Jackson quickly scuttled law enforcement as a potential career path: it was too rigid, too hierarchical. Crime scene would be a better fit for her skills, she thought, and so far it has been. Jackson doesn't want to move into the labs upstairs, to switch to DNA analysis or the fingerprint lab, even though she could make that choice as her career progresses. She wants to stay right here in crime scene. "Until I'm too old to be here," she says. There's just something about stepping into real people's lives, rooting through their cabinets, solving their intensely personal puzzles, that endlessly fascinates her.

MONDAYS ARE BUSY AT the crime scene office. Calls can come through so incessantly that Jackson loads up a car herself and heads out to help the rest of the team in the swamped districts. So far, tonight is quiet. A couple of shooting calls came through a few hours ago, during the day shift, and now we seem to be in the middle of a lull. Many of the techs are slumped around the office writing reports and waiting.

Almost simultaneously, Jackson and Harden announce that they are starving. Criminals don't exactly schedule a dinner break for the police, so you have to snack (and use the bathroom) when the opportunity presents itself. Technically, the team has a 10-code, police radio lingo used to describe crimes and alert one another of their whereabouts, for food breaks.

Harden blows a raspberry and rolls her eyes. "LOL," she says. "What is it, like 10-12?"

"I don't know, I've never used it," Jackson says, laughing.

Jackson breaks out a plastic container of multicolored Goldfish crackers. Harden perches with her hip on a desk and wolfs down a hot dog. Finally, a call comes over Jackson's radio, and the entire office perks up like meerkats.

"G3, G3, G3," the radio crackles.

A life spent working in a police department is a life spent responding viscerally to codes. G3 is an obscure one, instituted in Baltimore in 2018 to help officers respond more efficiently to clusters of violence. G3, short for "Grouping 3," means that whenever three shootings or homicides have occurred within a few hours, some of the people involved are likely to head out and retaliate. Sworn officers are to temporarily refrain from doing proactive work or attending low-level calls, and instead make themselves available to respond to the big stuff.

Officially, none of that affects the crime scene unit. All Jackson knows is that most evenings, unit 41, the night shift's head honcho over in the sworn division, announces G3 at some point or another. A shooting call usually comes through for crime scene soon afterward. When you've waited around at a desk for something to happen long enough, you develop a sort of clairvoyance about these things.

The techs pop out of their chairs and race to a computer-aided dispatch terminal to snoop before the full call goes out. *Whose district is it?* Is it a 2100, the last four digits of the homicide unit, and therefore code for murder? The evening's events march up a computer spreadsheet like trains on an arrivals board. Runaway; burglary; narcotics; disorderly; auto accident; family disturbance; hit and run.

"It's a shooooooting," Harden says in a singsong voice. "Oh wait, *fourteen* gunshots??"

Don't worry. It'll get worse.

3

SHOOTING

The rain comes down in salvos on a street that shines like vinyl in the headlights of a patrol car. The temperature has plummeted since the sun set and both Harden and Jackson are thankful for their baselayers. Incredibly, the fourteen suspected gunshots didn't result in a homicide, only a victim with a hole in his leg who is now at a nearby hospital. At the scene, bullet cases lie all over the place, mostly in a bristly thatch of grass in front of a clapboard duplex that looks like someone put a fist through its window.

Harden walks through this setting with one hand on a flashlight and the other at her side, a learned technique that prevents her from touching or adjusting anything she sees, which is verboten until she has thoroughly cataloged the scene. So far, the three officers who arrived first, about twenty or thirty minutes ago, have found eight spent cartridge cases, marking each with a miniature orange cone.

The officers tell Harden the details they've established by talking to the neighbors: the suspect stood by the duplex and shot at the victim as he fled up a sidewalk to a main road. One of the suspect's .45 caliber bullets is sitting in a puddle on a melamine chair. Another appears to be lodged in a tree.

Harden and Jackson stand in the drizzle, neither of them wearing their department-assigned rain jackets. Both consider them too bulky for work that requires twisting and crouching. Aiming their flashlights, they search for glitter in the grass.

"Oh wait, there's a casing right here, like almost under my feet," Jackson says.

"Ooh! And another one," Harden replies.

"Where?" one of the officers says, sweeping his flashlight along the ground.

I'm probably not supposed to be looking for the casings, but while they search, I can't help scanning the crabgrass in the play of their flashlight beams to find my own gleam of bronze. For a second I think I've got one, but it turns out to be the butt of a cigarillo.

Looking for stuff may not seem like a trainable skill, but it very much is. Since crime scene investigation became an in-demand career track in the early 2000s, new hires arrive with a better baseline than at any other time in history. Many have attended crime scene science classes that have popped up at universities (and even high schools) in recent years. But that was not always the case. Before the top level of the Baltimore division began their careers, in the 1990s or earlier, a tech often started straight after college, or even with a high school degree or GED, and would soon be required to perform meticulous tasks in accordance with rigorous procedure. This is how the "crime scene academy" began, a handing down of oral tradition.

Here in Baltimore, processing crime scenes on location remains an entry-level position. Salaries start at $50,000 a year.

When a technician receives an offer of employment, her first month on the job is spent training. In recent years, an outside instructor, a laconic, Oklahoma-based expert investigator named Everett Baxter Jr., has been flying in to teach a two-week training course based on his book *The Complete Crime Scene Investigation Handbook*. Baxter Jr.'s course follows the chapters, beginning with search and seizure rules, documentation, and evidence collection, then progressing to firearms, specialized evidence collection (bloodstain patterns, fire scenes), and strategies for inventorying injuries.

Most of the content was review for Harden—she'd been learning it for years. But she loved the hands-on practice—lifting prints in unusual ways, or taking footwear impressions on linoleum or sand. The modules were like lab exercises in science class, but more fun.

After the first two weeks, techs continue in the academy for the remainder of a month, familiarizing themselves with the cameras, practicing fingerprinting, and mastering any administrative tasks. One day, they all drive out to a towing lot called City Yard to practice dusting for prints on cars that aren't crime scenes. The last day, everyone takes a final exam and gets a certificate of completion. If there's time, KT Jaeger, the crime scene unit's director, orders pizza.

After new hires have passed competency exams for each skill, they move into a mentoring period, when they can ride along with senior technicians, or attend calls for lower-level offenses such as burglaries. They might assist experienced technicians by performing more forgiving tasks, such as taking photos or drawing sketches. Eventually, they work up to processing scenes themselves. There is no better way to get good at working crime scenes than to work more crime scenes, which is why a dedicated field staff, and in particular, a dedicated field staff in a crime-prone city, are some of the best around.

To LOCATE EVIDENCE IN the dark, sometimes you've got to shine your flashlight from an unexpected (or uncomfortable) angle. That's what the techs are doing now—Harden squatting for a low view and Jackson walking out into the street to come at the grass from the reverse. In the shafts of light, individual blades throw long shadows on the sidewalk. "Oh, one more!" Harden exclaims, and she's found another cartridge case, to the continued awe of the on-duty officers. The last couple were sitting open-end up in the grass, as impossible to see as dim holes in the dirt.

It is now full dark. Harden begins the photography portion of her duties by taking available light photos, which are one reason the techs learn advanced photography skills in their on-the-job training: she's got to shut off her flash, set her camera on a tripod, and hold the shutter open for a full second so that a jury can see how the scene appears in the natural nighttime lighting. The pictures will turn out too dark, but that's the point. Sometimes a lawyer will want to establish that a mugger could have been hiding in a doorway, or that a witness could clearly see a suspect's face. You don't get that kind of information when you light up a scene like a movie set.

Harden replaces the officers' cones with those yellow numbered triangles you see on every forensics show ("I think we all buy them from the same place," KT Jaeger says), then takes photos again. By now, the wind is gusting. It skitters one of the cartridge cases across the sidewalk.

"Ughhhh," Harden groans as she marches over to photograph the difference between where she originally placed the marker and the spot where the evidence moved. Annoying as it is, you're absolutely never allowed to pick evidence up and put it right back where it was before something—wind, snow, a car, a dog—moved it. Shifting evidence around, even for perfectly legitimate reasons, can lead to charges of tampering.

Instead of derailing the investigation, Harden documents the move, transfers the yellow marker to the case's new location, and then documents that. The photographs will back her up if she ever needs to explain her actions. One scene can require anywhere from ten to five hundred photographs, depending on how much evidence there is, but in general it is better to overshoot. You're not supposed to delete anything you take, even if you accidentally snap a pic of your shoe. *Where's picture number 51?* a lawyer might ask, and that's not a question you want to have to answer.

A 2011 academic paper that appeared in *Forensic Science Policy & Management* claimed that the best crime scene investigators are those who can apply critical thinking skills under adverse circumstances. Evidence that moves is a good example of that. You also have to adapt to considerable physical demands. In the four years that Jackson worked a district, she wriggled down storm drains to grab spent cartridges, climbed on roofs, and raced snowstorms. Cinese Caldwell, the crime scene unit's deputy director, once had to ride a cherry picker to an upstairs window to reach a body in a home whose back half had collapsed. Another pair of techs once retrieved a shot, burned body from a storm drain in Leakin Park, which writers for the *Baltimore Sun* have called the city's "largest unregistered graveyard."

Right now it's raining like hell. Harden works quickly to pack the found cartridge cases in individually labeled envelopes, and then to get the envelopes into the van. She doesn't want the wet cardstock to break open and spill the cases into an unmarked jumble. While Harden hustles, Jackson offers to sketch the scene, to create a sort of bird's-eye, real estate brochure view that is only required for crimes of sufficient seriousness and complexity. To make it, Jackson rolls a measuring device called a walking tape from a fixed point to each piece of evidence, noting the distances on her iPad, which she holds vertically so that it doesn't get soaked and glitchy. In her paramilitary clothing, she looks like a soldier pushing a child's toy lawn mower.

For the fixed point that anchors the sketch, Jackson chooses a street corner, because along with heights, obstructions, and weather, crime scene technicians also have to consider time. The technology involved in apprehending and convicting criminals changes constantly. Not only do technicians have to produce high-quality evidence for today's scientific capabilities, they also have to anticipate what a lab could need in twenty or thirty years. As the advent of DNA identification has shown, cases can be reopened and reprocessed decades into the future. The last thing you want is for an investigator in 2050 to come around asking whether the stop sign on which you based your sketch is now an Amazon housing unit or an autonomous bus stop or, well, whatever they'll have then.

THERE'S BEEN ANOTHER SHOOTING, this one on a multi-lane thoroughfare. And boy does this one look like a movie. The street has been blocked off from one major intersection clear down to another one hundred yards away. The glassy asphalt flashes neon every time the stoplights change from red to green. Wet crime scene tape flaps in the wind. Jackson lifts it to walk under.

Evidence is everywhere. A man was shot in the chest at one intersection and sprinted, covered in blood, almost to the other, where paramedics cut off his clothes to save him. Along the way, the wounded man passed through an unlocked car, shouting at the driver to get him to a hospital, then got out and charged into a restaurant. It's like a morbid Dr. Seuss rhyme: there's blood in the car, blood on the ground, blood on the clothes, blood in a sandwich shop. In a career in which the work varies hourly in complexity, this one is a project.

This shooting belongs to a pair of detectives, who are strolling, there's no other word for it, down the street under umbrellas. One is black. One is white. Both are wearing natty suits. The vignette is so film noir it's surprising no mournful jazz is playing in the background.

We are in a different district now, the Northern to Erika Harden's Southern. The technician who handles this area, a woman named Leah Garner, transitioned into crime scene investigation about two and a half years ago from a job in audiobook marketing and distribution for the BBC. She already had a degree in anthropology, so she went back to school to pick up a few more science classes, taking on a gig as a police dispatcher to make money while she did it.

The dispatcher job was tough: An unending onslaught of requests for help left zero room for error. Garner felt like she had to be on high alert for days at a time, so that no one would die because she underperformed. It did something to her ability to empathize, she says. "I found myself judging and really wondering if people in general would ever make better choices or 'fix their own problems,' which I know sounds really awful," she says. But she is not alone: Compassion fatigue and burnout are common in public service careers, police dispatching and crime scene investigation included. Garner welcomed the shift to crime scene. She hoped the slower pace, increased control, and greater sense of closure—she could find out the resolution of a case if she wanted—would help her get back to her compassionate self.

In the hour she's been here, Garner has peppered the block with evidence markers—a number "1" for the cartridge case at one end of the street, and letters next to the clothes and shoes and bloodstains and general detritus. She still has a mountain of work ahead of her. She'll need to take swabs of the blood from the restaurant's door handle, photos of both sides of the car, a sketch of the whole block. A peanut gallery of restaurant staff stands around, asking can they walk through this door or that one, complaining about the effect of the shooting on their business. What keeps her going, Garner says, is wanting justice for victims, not putting anyone through a second ordeal at the hands of police. If she can walk through that particular hell for people, she says, the hard work is worth it. It's certainly better than answering the phone.

While Garner works, one of the detectives strolls over.

They make conversation for a minute, and he ends with: "What a night for all this to go down, huh?" He disappears in the direction of his car, his pant legs damp where his umbrella's protection ends.

Jackson and Garner continue working in the rain. Forty-five minutes later, they drive back to the bay, where Garner seals her paper bags of dry evidence across the back with blue tape marked "evidence." She plugs her iPad into a printer that pops out stickers displaying the major facts of the case and sticks those on the front. The door to Evidence Control, a subdivision at headquarters that houses crime-related objects until they're needed for analysis or court, is card-locked, so she uses her ID to walk through to an attendant at the counter. There were no guns at the scene, so she has nothing to place inside the locked mailbox designated to safely hold firearms until a crime lab assistant takes them up to the lab in the morning.

The drenched shirt and shoes can't be submitted to evidence control as-is. Garner places these in a drying cabinet, one of several glass-fronted, lockable booths in the bay that blows filtered air over wet items to prevent mold or mildew from growing on them and mucking up any biological clues. These gadgets are de rigueur for crime scene field teams. Fungal contaminants are a scourge. Garner logs the items in the drying cabinet on a chain of custody sheet; she'll update it when she removes the items during her shift tomorrow and submits them to evidence control then.

While Garner logs the evidence, Rebecca Jackson goes back up to the office, writes her reports for the cases she's worked, places those in the drawer for review, and unloads all of her equipment from the SUV so it will be ready for the morning shift. She finally gets a chance to eat the dinner she brought to work, then drives the hour-long commute back to her home in Eastern Maryland. When she arrives, her hound mix, Red, trots out of the dark bowels of her house to meet her at the door, like he always does.

Erika Harden yawns. Shivering makes her tired, and she still has a lot of work to do. Tomorrow afternoon, she has to be in the office early to prepare for the trial of a case she worked forever ago. At her desk, decorated with photos and graphics of the Joker from *Batman*, she looks at old photographs to jog her memory. This particular case had required more fortitude than most: a man who'd been set up by a prostitute and murdered by the prostitute's boyfriend had been left to rot in an apartment in the July heat. When they'd opened the door, the stench hit them like a wall. Harden would never retch into a bush—"that would be embarrassing," she says—but she still put on an N95 mask with a charcoal filter. All it did was keep the flies off her face. She still had to breathe through her mouth.

There was so much to do at that scene—making sketches, taking photographs, and collecting evidence—that Harden had requested a backup investigator to help. They worked side by side for five hours next to a body that was so decomposed, she whispers, "he looked like his ass-hole was falling out."

4

HISTORY

You used to be able to get away with anything. *Really* anything. John Mulaney, the comedian and former *Saturday Night Live* writer, has a whole bit about it. "Here's how easy it was to get away with bank robbery back in the thirties," goes his joke. "As long as you weren't still *there* when the police arrived, you had a ninety-nine percent chance of getting away with it."

If the 1930s were embarrassing for law enforcement, the 1800s were the third panel of Hieronymus Bosch's *Garden of Earthly Delights*, complete with torture chambers and pigs in nun habits. Robbers, frauds, and counterfeiters had long, illustrious careers. Horse thieves commandeered a whole valley in Nevada. In Labette County, Kansas, a fake family now known as "The Bloody Benders" robbed and murdered at least ten, and maybe as many as twenty-one, travelers who passed by their trailside home, bashing their heads in with a hammer when they weren't looking. When the local authorities finally came by to investigate, the Benders simply disappeared, leaving nearly a dozen bodies in the backyard.

To be fair to the watchmen and the gendarmes and the pre–twentieth century sheriffs, they tried. As early as the phrase "to have blood on your hands" appeared in the vernacular, there had been a sense that crimes marked people, and that *stuff* left over after a crime occurred could link victims to their assailants. Investigators collected clothing, photographs, shoe prints, letters, bullets, and delivery vehicles for suspected poisons (cups, cakes) to produce at trials. Even deep in the country, if a dead body showed up, someone would usually press a medical doctor into service to examine it.

Unfortunately, or fortunately, depending on what side of which law you're on, policing had not yet grown into the indefatigable panopticon it would become. Procedures were left not just to individual agencies but often to individual enforcers, and criminals slipped through cracks all the time. Part of the problem was that methods for identifying humans were unreliable at best. Names and addresses could be changed, appearances altered. Forget solving every crime, a police agency prior to 1880 couldn't even keep track of criminals it had already apprehended. In the Wild West, a new mustache and an interstate move was as good as the FBI Witness Protection Program.*

Like most scientific revolutions, the rise of criminalistics was not the work of one person, but a zeitgeist that swept contemporary thought in chemistry, biology, physics, medicine, anthropology, and sociology. In the early nineteenth century, impulses toward penal reform had blossomed into the relatively new field of criminology, in which skepticism and reason were replacing traditionally religious views on behavior.

By the end of that same century, Europe was in the grip of a rapid industrialization that had improved almost every measurable aspect of daily existence, with swift transportation, electric lighting, and telegraph-based communication becoming commonplace. Refrigeration made the preservation of bodies after death more palatable, and more medical examiners were performing autopsies. Doctors and academics began to wonder if science couldn't solve crime

---

* The historic need to identify individuals is one reason one of the most influential industry organizations in forensics, founded in 1915, is called the IAI—the International Association for Identification.

the same way it had everything else.

The transformation began advancing all over the continent. In 1876, an Italian psychiatrist named Cesare Lombroso put forth a system of criminal identification based on the templates of anthropology and the writings of Charles Darwin. Lombroso's positivist school held that criminals existed at a lower level of evolution than non-criminals. They were, in fact, a subclass of humans, and therefore possessed physical defects, termed "stigmata." The stigmata, traits common to non-white races or forms of physical ugliness, were supposed to be outward markers of inner deviance that police could use to identify born criminals.

This was, of course, pseudoscience. By arguing that criminals were born, not made, positivism created a framework for racists to claim that any physical traits they didn't like marked a person as a danger to society. The school of thought contributed mightily to arguments in favor of forced sterilization, unjust incarceration, and even Nazi eugenics. Thankfully, positivism, alongside its psychological twin, phrenology, a practice which claimed to be able to analyze people's minds based on the bumps on their skulls, was eventually discredited.

While positivism continued to hold sway, a police department records clerk in Paris invented a more realistic human measuring system. The clerk, Alphonse Bertillon, realized that while one unusually sized body part might not uniquely identify a person, a collection of them could. His system, anthropometry, or *Bertillonage*, involved measuring enough of a person's immutable physical characteristics, including the size of the head and body and the shape of the ears and eyes, that he could differentiate individuals. (He also included photos—face-on and profile—in what were the first-ever mug shots). Anthropometry was massively successful. In 1884, Bertillon used it to identify 241 criminals who had ended up in the police station more than once. Police forces in Great Britain, Europe, and the Americas soon adopted his system.

In the 1890s, the field of forensic science exploded. The second of Europe's twin "rippers"—France's Joseph Vacher—began terrorizing the countryside around Lyon in 1894, stabbing, raping, and mutilating young women and boys. Lyon was, at that time, a lodestar in the burgeoning field of legal medicine. The head of the Institute of Legal Medicine at the University of Lyon, a physician, professor, and criminologist named Alexandre Lacassagne, was performing regular feats of biological wizardry for local law enforcement. By studying cadavers, skeletons, and scientific papers, Lacassagne had learned to determine age and height from pieces of bone; to assess whether a body had been moved based on splotches on the skin; and to guess at death-causing injuries based on the condition of the lungs and throat cartilage, among many other skills.

Today, medical forensics is almost a wholly independent operation from crime scene investigation, but in the early days, the boundaries were blurred. The most serious crimes involved bodies, and bodies were the province of doctors. If the police wanted information about how a murder had been committed, they required someone with knowledge of rigor mortis, lividity, body positions, and other death-related phenomena to explain what had happened. Besides, doctoring had been in existence for most of human history, far longer than many of the contemporary sciences. It was the smartest place to start.

There is a fantastic book about the birth of medical forensics in France, *The Killer of Little Shepherds* by Douglas Starr, that tells the story of Alexandre Lacassagne. In it, Starr describes how Lacassagne established that the serial killer Vacher was mentally competent to stand trial. "To the professor, the entire progression of crimes, despite their perversity, indicated the kind of planning and presence of mind that only a sane man could possess," Starr writes. Using bloodstains and injury patterns, Lacassagne re-created Vacher's murders to the point that he felt he could prove that Vacher was acting methodically, and that he knew right from wrong. "Vacher was, to put it simply, a criminal."

As brilliant as Lacassagne and the medical investigators were, they were not alone in pursuing criminals by scientific means. In Austria in the 1890s, crimes were adjudicated by examining justices, or *untersuchungsrichter*, who functioned as investigators, prosecutors, and judges. One of these, Hans Gross, worked in the regional court in Graz, Austria, where he had begun to tire of witnesses who lied, forgot important details, or had ulterior motives for denouncing the accused. Hoping to establish an objective "testimony of physical things," he began collecting case studies of crimes for a textbook.

Gross released his book, *Handbuch für Untersuchungsrichter als System der Kriminalististik*, later translated as "Criminal Investigation: A Practical Handbook for Magistrates, Police Officers, and Lawyers," in 1893. It was comprehensive, covering witness interviews, common weapons, crime scene sketching, the use of subject matter experts, found blood and footprints, and even superstitions about dead bodies. The book blazed through the legal establishment, becoming reprinted in a dozen languages. Almost single-handedly, it established the "crime scene" as a specific entity in space and time, to be investigated using appropriate practices.[*]

Law enforcement agencies were eager to apply the new disciplines to fighting real crimes, but labs existed at universities, not in police departments. That the police would eventually maintain their own labs was thanks to Edmond Locard, a flat-faced, wild-haired polymath who also hailed from Lyon, France. Born in 1877, Locard was thirteen when forensic science became an international phenomenon. He embarked on a strenuous career of study with every great mind of early criminalistics he could find. After earning his medical doctorate in 1902, he assisted Lacassagne at the University of Lyon, earned a law degree, and partnered with Bertillon in Paris to study his identification system.

In the early 1900s, when Locard returned home from vis-

---

[*] An interesting aside: Hans Gross's son, Otto Gross, became an anarchist, drug addict, and well-known psychoanalyst who was at one point treated by both Sigmund Freud and Carl Jung. In 1913, Hans had Otto, who had a history of schizophrenia, arrested, removed from Germany, and committed to a hospital in Austria. Some believe this event influenced the novel *The Trial*, by Otto's friend Franz Kafka.

iting police stations and criminologists all over the world, his pastel riverside hometown was a hotbed of criminal activity. The Lyon police were desperate to control the melee. They granted Locard two rooms in an attic of the local courthouse to open the first police station crime lab in the world. There, he focused on what would today be called "trace" evidence—hairs, fibers, shoe prints, dust—and blood.

Alphonse Bertillon, the inventor of Bertillonage and the mug shot, was at one time so internationally famous that Sir Arthur Conan Doyle namechecked him in his Sherlock Holmes novel *The Hound of the Baskervilles*.* But Locard quickly surpassed him, becoming known as the "Sherlock Holmes of France." In fact, Locard was not so dissimilar from the fictional detective. Highly educated, he played the violin, and undertook meticulous hobbies such as stamp collecting. In some ways, he imitated Holmes on purpose: after reading the first Sherlock Holmes novel, 1887's *A Study in Scarlet*, in which Holmes claims to be able to identify 140 varieties of cigar ash, Locard conducted and published his

---

* A client arrives at Holmes's office, requesting the "second highest expert" on crime scene investigation in Europe. Miffed, Holmes asks who could possibly be the first. "To the man of precisely scientific mind the work of Monsieur Bertillon must always appeal strongly," the client says. Ouch.

own study on the forensic value of dirt and grime. He titled it: "The Analysis of Dust Traces (in three parts)." Part one alone contains a two-page list of cruds particular to various occupations.

Like his fictional counterpart, Locard was also fond of expounding on crime-solving in a more philosophical sense. In his book *L'enquête Criminelle et les Méthodes Scientifiques* ("The Criminal Investigation and Scientific Methods"), published in 1920, he introduced an idea that became so fundamental to forensic science it's one of the first things modern crime scene investigators learn in school. Today, it is known as Locard's Principle: any time people, items, and places come into contact, some small trace will be left behind on each. "The truth is that none can act with the intensity induced by criminal activities without leaving multiple traces of his path," he wrote (in French).

He didn't add, "The game is afoot, my dear Watson." But it fits.

OVER THE NEXT CENTURY the field of crime scene investigation expanded as it borrowed techniques from other maturing sciences. Ballistics blew up (pardon the pun) after one of the most infamous crimes in American history, 1929's St. Valentine's Day Massacre, in which four unidentified men—two of them dressed as police officers—lined up seven members of a Chicago bootlegging gang against a wall, and shot them dozens of times.

The man tasked with investigating the crime, Herman Bundesen, was Chicago's health inspector and coroner, but functioned more as a publicity-hungry vigilante, concocting public health initiatives and staging photo ops with a bald-faced aim toward making the papers. With the press reporting on Chicago's crime epidemic daily, Bundesen appointed a "blue ribbon" grand jury made up of six leading businessmen and officials to help sort through evidence from the massacre scene.

One of the grand jury members, vice president of Colgate-Palmolive-Peet Company Burt Massee, had heard about a man who had presented ballistics evidence in the appeals trial of anarchists Nicola Sacco and Bartolomeo Vanzetti, a sensationalist case that had made the news across the country. Concerned for his business in Chicago's corrupt atmosphere, Massee convinced another member of the panel, Walter Olson, president of the Olson Rug Company, to use their combined money to hire the Sacco and Vanzetti ballistics master for their own case. Perhaps such an expert could restore honor to their city.

The ballistics expert was Calvin Goddard, a former Army Medical Corps major who, while working as the administrative director of the Cornell University Clinic in New York City, transformed his boyhood hobby—guns—into a calling. By playing with medical equipment designed to peek into the bladder and throat, he examined the insides of gun barrels, finding imperfections in the spiral grooves, firing pins, and extraction mechanisms that would leave unique markings on bullets and their spent cases. One of his developments, a comparison microscope that would allow an examiner to look at two bullet cases simultaneously, made him so famous that he quit the clinic to establish the Bureau of Forensic Ballistics with a judge who had spent ten years collecting measurements from every pistol factory he could find. A version of this microscope is still in use today.

Goddard agreed to come out to Chicago, and while he never solved the St. Valentine's Day Massacre, he did rule out the involvement of police weapons, eventually tying evidence from the scene to guns found in the home of gangster Fred "Killer" Burke. More important for the field of forensic science, he established the first police-independent

Scientific Crime Detection Laboratory in the United States on the campus of Northwestern University's Law School. The FBI used it as a model when it opened its own crime lab in 1932.

By far the most significant upheaval in crime scene science was the introduction of DNA fingerprinting. And Leicester University researcher Alec Jeffreys remembers exactly when it happened. At 9:05 a.m. on Monday, September 10, 1984, Jeffreys returned to a study he'd been running over the weekend on the heritability of family traits to find that his work was ruined.

In his previous research, Jeffreys had discovered that certain places on the genome were highly variable. In these places, which he called "minisatellites" (the forensic community now calls them loci), the genetic code repeated between two and dozens of times, forming a sort of stutter that could be measured. One person's code might say TCTA TCTA TCTA TCTA, for example—a four—while another's would go on to repeat twenty times. Jeffreys's team had been hoping to track whether these repeats were heritable, passing down through generations. Instead, each person's pattern appeared to be unique, a random combination of the repeat counts of his or her parents.

At first, Jeffreys thought he'd have to throw out his experiment ("this is too complicated," he thought), but he and the rest of his team quickly realized that a profile made up of the different lengths of repeats could be useful. Like Bertillon's system of body dimensions, genetic repeat counts collected from enough locations could serve as an identifier, a DNA fingerprint. Over the next two days, Jeffreys cut himself and left his own blood all over the laboratory, hoping to test whether the DNA in it would remain intact enough for the analysis after it dried. It did.

In 1986, Jeffreys had the first opportunity to apply his discovery to a criminal case: police from the English county of Leicestershire called about two fifteen-year-old girls— Dawn Ashworth and Lynda Mann—who had been raped and murdered. Under questioning, a seventeen-year-old boy with learning disabilities named Richard Buckland had confessed to the killing of Ashworth, whom he knew. He refused to admit to killing Mann. The police, hoping to find Buckland guilty of both murders, asked if Jeffreys could incriminate him using his new genetic-profiling technology.

Buckland, as it turned out, was innocent. Although the DNA from semen found in Mann matched that found in Ashworth, the profile didn't match Buckland's. Police released Buckland, but now they had nothing. With few clues and the murderer still at large, they established a genetic dragnet, requesting blood samples from all local men aged seventeen to thirty-four. Nothing matched. After eight months, the police had investigated more than five thousand samples and still had no leads.

And then a man came forward with a story he'd heard at a local pub. A coworker named Ian Kelly had admitted to falsifying his test, giving his own blood to the police on behalf of a young father named Colin Pitchfork. Pitchfork had wanted not to be tested so badly, he'd doctored his passport and made up a story that *he'd* already given blood for someone else. Police arrested both men, and Pitchfork soon confessed. When Jeffreys ran his procedure on Pitchfork's blood, the DNA fingerprint matched the semen found in both girls. Pitchfork was sentenced to life in prison. Alec Jeffreys was knighted.

The forensic community rallied behind DNA fingerprinting, calling it the future. In 1994, the U.S. Congress passed the DNA Identification Act, which allowed the FBI to expand a pilot project they'd been working on since Jeffreys's discovery, a system of databases known as CODIS, or Combined DNA Index System. CODIS standardized the

DNA fingerprint Jeffreys had discovered, requiring every police jurisdiction to upload the genetic stutters (the official name is short tandem repeats, or STRs) from the same thirteen gene locations. (In 2017, the FBI added seven more, for a total of twenty.) Police departments could upload DNA from crime scenes, convicted offenders, missing persons, and unidentified human remains, and search for connections between any or all of them.

CODIS was, finally, the fullest realization of the dreams of early European criminalists—a directory that could objectively link crimes to criminals, keep track of people, and rule out the innocent. It revolutionized crime and punishment—made it so much more difficult to get away with bad behavior that serious rapes and murders are now often national news. It would have been convenient for law enforcement if it hadn't taken a century to figure out how to do it. But hey, that's science.

5

FORENSIC BIOLOGY

Bang Bang Bang Bang!

Rana DellaRocco is ebulliently describing her average day at the office, but I can't concentrate because someone is firing a gun. I try to peek down at street level from her eighth-floor window, expecting pandemonium, but all I see is a finger of Baltimore's inner harbor and the gold and verdigris tip of the historic Bank of America Building. DellaRocco continues talking as if nothing has happened, her dirty blond shag swaying in the sunlight. "If there haven't been any high-profile crimes," she says, "I answer emails for seven hundred hours, and then I go to about a thousand meetings."

Though many, many women make up the base levels of crime scene investigation, the rooms and round tables at the top of the industry remain occupied mostly by men. But in her twenty-two years at the Baltimore Police Department, Rana DellaRocco has earned herself a seat. The head of Baltimore's forensic laboratory section, she oversees the in-house processing of every piece of evidence that moves through this department. Her office, which she has painstakingly worked her way up to, sits beneath the firearms lab. That's where the gunshots are coming from.

A native daughter of Baltimore, DellaRocco didn't have a moment when she knew she wanted to solve crimes. She didn't measure bay water in graduated cylinders or pester her parents to buy her a Sherlock Holmes deerstalker cap for the relatively mild winters or anything. She was, simply, a classic overachiever, so delighted to read books that she brought them to parties in high school. She got to the top the way both girls and forensic scientists tend to: by being very, very smart; and by working very, very hard.

DellaRocco, I should point out, looks like an actress playing a police administrator in a TV show, down to the wide smile and the well-cut blazer. She laughs readily and is as friendly as a golden retriever. On a chair in her office sits a ballcap her coworkers bought her that says CHEERTATER on it, a play on the "Cheer-o-cracy" scene from the movie *Bring It On*. A common thing that happens in DellaRocco's office: she will get stuck in an expansive conversation with coworkers, talking and laughing, and have to shoo people out for her next appointment.

DellaRocco happily calls herself a dork, and like many who work in the labs, she majored in biology. (The rest usually go for chemistry.) Pursuing a career in science was a conscious choice. She considered taking the liberal arts, juris doctor route, but felt like she would end up bored and frustrated in a law office somewhere, pushing paper and playing with words. Why would she do that to herself if she could pursue a topic that would actually keep her brain occupied?

While DellaRocco was in school, she picked up a part-time gig at a private psychiatric hospital. She chose the place because her mother worked there, the hours were flexible, and the pay was solid enough to help out with car payments and gas. She never intended the job to be any more of a career path than her other side gig, slinging costume jewelry in the mall. But, as overachievers do, she accidentally made herself indispensable. By the time she graduated, DellaRocco was doing general "Gal Friday stuff" for the hospital administrator's executive assistant, including printing materials for accreditation. She worked as a patient advocate in disputes with doctors.

But God, she was bored. So bored that every day during the receptionist's lunch break she would borrow the hospital's copy of the *Baltimore Sun* and scan the classifieds for a gig that might be more interesting. A listing for Crime Laboratory Technician at the Baltimore Police Department caught her interest. Assuming it was a lab job, DellaRocco applied. Working in a police department sounded like just the thing.

The interview was in the same building her office is in now—the Bishop L. Robinson Sr. Police Administration

Building,* a concrete monument to crime and punishment about four blocks from Baltimore's inner harbor. Back then, forensic science was just beginning to assume solid form as a police discipline. The questions weren't organized or formal—but the interview did take place in front of a panel of three crime scene supervisors, all men. DellaRocco nervously sat across from them. She'd never been great at interviews.

The supervisors explained the job. Was it boring? No. Was it a lab job? Also no. "I was like, oh wait, this is to go *out* to crime scenes?" DellaRocco says. No doubt finding her naivete hilarious, one of the interviewers gave her a deadpan "yeeeeah." DellaRocco thought, *Okay, well, whatever! Let's see what* that's *like.*

Nothing's fast in law enforcement. It is common for months to pass between interviewing for a position and being offered a job, with zero contact in between, and this is what happened to DellaRocco. Radio silence for a full year after she interviewed. Then an unexpected call on a Tuesday. "They were like, *Do you want to come to crime scene school? It starts on Monday,*" she says.

DellaRocco missed the first two weeks of crime scene

---

* Named for Baltimore's first African American police commissioner, Bishop Robinson, who served from 1984 to 1987.

academy because she felt obligated to give the psychiatric hospital two weeks' notice. But once she got started, she adored the work. Compared to the hospital, the action was nonstop. It was an extrovert's dream, people-watching on steroids: You walked straight into strangers' houses and you never, ever knew what you were going to see. To this day, DellaRocco considers working crime scenes the "best job ever." Many of the techs in the mobile unit agree. Several told me they're never leaving, no matter how many children they have or how exhausting the late nights get. The job is just too weird, and too great, to give up.

But DellaRocco also wanted to be the best, and she still had her sights set on a lab job. A few years after she joined the Baltimore PD, a grant arrived that provided money for her to study in the forensic labs during her off-hours, provided she did it in addition to her regular gig. She jumped at the opportunity, putting in a full shift collecting evidence, then posting up in the serology lab, where she spent a second half-shift every day screening evidence for semen, blood, and saliva. Before she could switch over to the labs completely, she had to finish six months of training, then wait for the crime scene unit to hire a replacement. Nine months later, she was a serologist.

There was a time when a crime scene investigator could

be a generalist, someone who went to crime scenes and then returned to the department to analyze everything she found—blood, bullets, hair, fingerprints, whatever. Now, it is virtually impossible to do it all. As science has grown more sophisticated, an investigator would have to be proficient in so many techniques across so many conceptual fields that people simply specialize. The areas of expertise get so granular that forensic analysts at the top of their field, including DellaRocco, collect master's degrees and professional certifications like stats on baseball cards. DellaRocco's include a master's degree in forensic serology and DNA from the University of Florida College of Pharmacy; and, as of 2019, a master's in public administration from the University of Baltimore.

Here's why specialization is important: at the Baltimore Police Department, serology has been folded into a forensic biology office that functions as a triage station, sorting and distributing incoming evidence so that it can be processed in the most logical order. If, say, a gun shows up here, you might start by testing it for blood—and there are a dozen different ways to do that. Generally, a biologist would swab any of the gun's textured areas, such as the handgrip, with a cotton-tipped applicator, leaving the smooth areas untouched for fingerprint analysis. She would save a piece of the swab for the DNA team (another set of specialists), then treat another piece with leucomalachite green, a chemical that reacts with blood's oxygen-carrying hemoglobin to turn blue.

That's the first pass. Leucomalachite green is a "presumptive" test—quick and easy, but not completely exclusionary. To confirm human blood, the biologist would next place a bit of the swab on an ABAcard HemaTrace, which operates like an old-school pregnancy test. If human blood is present, two lines will appear. If it's rust or chocolate sauce or wine or dirt, you'll only get one.

The detectives who are investigating a crime advise the forensic biology office on which tests they need, so let's say our hypothetical detective makes a trip up to the tenth floor to request that this hypothetical gun also be tested for semen. The biologist would begin with an initial test for acid phosphatase, an enzyme that occurs in male and female sexual fluids. She would confirm the result by testing for p30, an enzyme specific to semen, or by swiping the sample on a slide and staining that with a pair of chemicals nicknamed "Christmas tree stain" because they color sperm heads red and their tails green. Would a forensic analyst have time to do all that, go to crime scenes, shoot off ballistics evidence, compare fingerprints, track the life spans of blowflies, *and* create a bloodstain pattern analysis art project out of red string?

"Even the detectives here are like, don't you just put it in the machine and then the answer comes out?" DellaRocco says.

But yeah, no.

In addition to blood and semen, the forensic biology lab in Baltimore tests incoming evidence for hidden fingerprints, which are called latent fingerprints because *latent* is Latin for "hidden." They have, for example, a cyanoacrylate fuming chamber that shoots vaporized superglue at prints you cannot see. The superglue adheres to moisture and leaves a permanent white film that can be dusted or stained with dye. It's one of a dozen methods that can resurface latent prints, several others of which are practiced here as well. Maybe the coolest is the lab's latest project, a vacuum metal deposition (VMD) machine, which sprays nanoscale-thin layers of gold and zinc onto suspected fingerprints on surfaces as thin as tissue paper. The resulting metal smudges show where clothing or other difficult-to-fingerprint items have been touched, so analysts know where to swab it for DNA.

DNA is more complicated yet.

While working in the labs is generally less harrowing than processing crime scenes on location, sometimes it gets gnarly in here as well. Forensic biology analysts don't process bodies, but the medical examiner's office is forever sending over shower curtains a partially decomposed body was wrapped in, or clothes found on dead people floating in Baltimore's myriad lakes, bays, and rivers. "It can get really disgusting in here," says Dana Keiter, Baltimore's current serology technical lead, who took over a few people after DellaRocco. She wears her hair in a little mohawk.

One time, Keiter had to process a big green city trash can in which a murderer had dumped a body. It was the middle of the summer, and the corpse had been left to rot in a vacant house for days. By the time detectives discovered it, maggots were crawling in and out of the can. It was full of juices. "It was so hot, the body was melting," Keiter says, as if that's the kind of thing people say.

A human corpse smells unlike anything else on Earth, a fetid combination of rotten musk, microwaved broccoli, and spoiled dairy. Analysts in the forensic bio lab refer to this aroma as "decomp." Keiter didn't even want to bring the trash can up to the lab, where the smell would linger for at least the rest of the day (they're not allowed to use Febreze in here). She ended up processing it down in the bay, wearing two layers of gowns and gloves, a face mask, and eye protection. She looked like an astronaut.

"Everything was covered," she says. "Everything."

IN THE EARLY 2000S, DNA forensics were only beginning to become standardized practice throughout the country. The FBI had rolled out the national level of their CODIS database in 1998, and Baltimore had just established a unit to process DNA in-house, purchasing much of the new equipment with money from a National Institute of Justice grant. This was a blessing for DellaRocco, who now had the opportunity to move seamlessly from serology into DNA, training under the first-ever technical lead, who had come from a private lab specializing in paternity testing. She applied for a master's program in the topic, a low-residency, online option at the University of Florida. The timing was perfect.

Though DNA remains the gold standard in forensic science, the labs in which it is processed look like any other:

a series of rooms, mostly white and gray, in which hulking, multithousand-dollar machines squat on thick countertops. Some of these machines, toaster oven–looking things packed with some of the most impressive science on Earth, take a minuscule amount of material from a crime scene and extract the useful part, washing and washing the sample with various chemicals until nothing remains but pure DNA.

Wary of contamination, the analysts move their samples from toaster oven to toaster oven in little tubes. The machines crack the DNA open, amplify just those fragments necessary for comparison by doubling them over and over, then separate the fragments by length. The output comes in what's called an electropherogram, a bar graph of Alec Jeffreys's genetic repeats, laid out fragment by fragment. Each fragment shows up as two measurements, one from a person's mother and one from his father (these are called "alleles," which you may remember from that high school biology lecture about Gregor Mendel and the peas). An analyst can compare two electropherograms, from a suspect and from a crime scene, for example, and say, *Okay, this fragment's got a seven and a fourteen. Does that match?* By the time an analyst has matched both alleles at, let's say the twenty-two genetic locations the Baltimore PD currently uses as a standard, the chances that you've got the wrong guy are astronomical.

DellaRocco worked in the DNA and serology labs for twelve years before getting called up to the deputy director position. In that time, she finally found a subject that would satisfy her endless curiosity. DNA technology changes so rapidly people compare it to Moore's law in microchips: power doubles every two years. While DellaRocco worked, the genetic analyzers got faster and faster—a 310 became a 3100 became a 3130 became a 3500. The chemistry protocol changed five times. By 2014, DellaRocco and the lab were working at the bleeding edge of DNA science. She pushed for the unit to adopt a new technology called probabilistic genotyping, a method that could solve one of the most ethically challenging problems forensic DNA scientists face: mixtures.

It is rare that only one person has touched an item from a crime scene. When several people have, and their cells are processed together, their genetic repeats become inextricably combined. This is a mixture, and it can be a problem. While the odds of nailing the wrong person are infinitesimal in a one-to-one comparison, a crime scene sample that has been touched by multiple people is much less conclusive.

As an illustration, let's say DNA from a knife shows up with four stutter counts at a single genetic location. If the counts are 4, 12, 15, and 42, ten possible genetic profiles (4,4; 12,12; 15,15; 42,42; 4,12; 4,15; 4,42; 12,15; 12,42; and 15,42) could have contributed to it. Worse, different DNA scientists calculate match statistics very differently, so a given match could seem reasonable—or highly unlikely—just based on who does the math.

Greg Hampikian, a biologist at Boise State University who founded the Idaho Innocence Project at the school, has helped overturn more than thirty wrongful DNA convictions internationally. He compares unscrambling DNA mixtures to putting the letters of two people's names into a jar and trying to pull only those two names back out. One time he tried it with his own name and the name of a prosecutor he was trying to convince and managed to spell Al Gore, Porky Pig, Larry King, Mary Kay, Happy Gilmore, King Phillip, and King Lear (among others).

Probabilistic genotyping, the technology DellaRocco wanted to adopt, attempts to fix this problem. It employs statistics and math to sort out which measurements belong in the same genome, cleaving a blend into individual people. When Baltimore started playing around with it, the public defender's office came down on the forensic bio unit hard, wanting to know how reliable the method they were using was, and recommending that they invest in modeling programs that would make their conclusions more resistant to ambiguity. "I was like, okay, yeah, you're right. We should. Let's do that," DellaRocco says. They went with TrueAllele, a program that removes the need for human analysts to interpret the data in ways that might be subjective. (Hampikian is a fan.) By the time they had it up and running, Baltimore was the sixth lab in the world to use it.

So far, DNA fingerprinting has resisted the kinds of scandals that have mortified other subspecialties of crime scene expertise (bite mark analysis, for example, which came into fashion in the 1940s and was discarded as junk science in the 2010s). But DNA is hardly immune to mistakes. In 2015, Hampikian patented an artificial DNA sequence, a "nullomer," that doesn't occur in nature. It responds exceptionally well to the DNA amplification process, creating a huge, obvious band in an electropherogram. Hampikian hopes police departments will one day add it to all DNA samples taken from suspects at a station as a precaution. If the oversize nullomer band ever appears in a sample from a crime scene, DNA scientists will know immediately that the sample has been contaminated.

That's easy enough, but some of the next-generation DNA analysis methods are so sci-fi it would be helpful to set up a consult with Isaac Asimov to navigate their ethical consequences. "The community is moving in a way that's a little scary to me," DellaRocco says, pointing out a next-gen genetic sequencer in the corner that could perform some of the most boundary-pushing science possible. The sequencer looks the same as anything else in the room—like a desktop washing machine. Only it's dark. It's not yet being used for casework.

The next-gen sequencer, when in operation, can supersede Alec Jeffreys's stutter counts entirely, mapping the DNA within the repeated fragments, or searching the whole genome for single nucleotide polymorphisms, or SNPs, instead. SNPs are little mutations in individual genes that are sometimes associated with particular traits. Analyzing these would provide law enforcement agencies with information they could use to reverse engineer a person's physical appearance from genetic code. From DNA found on, say, the handgrip of a gun, authorities can already predict eye color, hair color, ancestry—and, some claim, even face shape—of a potential assailant. Companies such as Parabon NanoLabs, which offers the service to help police departments narrow suspect lists, call this new technology DNA phenotyping, from "phenotype," the genetics term for a creature's observable characteristics.

Today, DellaRocco rarely gets to process a maggot-filled trash can or play with the DNA sequencer herself, the classic problem of ascending into management only to have your job description change entirely. But she remains absurdly driven. In addition to overseeing Baltimore's entire analysis section, she teaches at Towson University, Stevenson University, and Loyola University. Once a year, she travels to another crime lab somewhere in the world to audit (and observe and potentially adopt) their methods. Through some alchemy of space and time, she also has three teenage children, just bought a new house, and has perfectly polished bloodred fingernails.

When I emailed DellaRocco to ask how she does so many things at once, she replied—immediately—with a numbered list of her strategies: She uses the calendar on her phone as a personal assistant. She lets literally no minute go to waste. She subscribes to the "argument of the growing heap," which claims that no one coin makes you rich or one cupcake makes you overweight, but that at some point, one last coin or one last cupcake absolutely will. "So, every coin and every cupcake counts," DellaRocco said. "Getting a degree doesn't feel that daunting because every class hour, every paper adds to the growing heap that will be your degree. Every action toward some goal counts."

Who thinks like that?

6

DRUGS

Rana DellaRocco and I left her office and walked up to the drug lab. Then we walked right past its first door, a wet lab she won't let me enter.

"It's the fentanyl," she says. "It's transdermal. If it touches your skin or you breathe it in, even two little grains of it can kill you."

Baltimore transitioned from a town addicted to heroin to a fentanyl nightmare around 2015, in a shift that announced itself first on the streets. Over the years, many Baltimore area drug users had learned to manage their addictions to heroin, using enough to avoid withdrawal but not enough to overdose. Then one day the heroin wasn't heroin anymore. It was fentanyl, a synthetic painkiller that can be one hundred times more powerful than morphine. Chemical lightning. Patrol officers began carrying NARCAN, a nasal spray that can reverse an opioid overdose, to revive people slumped anywhere and everywhere. People who thought they knew what they were doing were dropping dead all over the city.

After beat police and Baltimore's addicted population, the next people to watch the fentanyl crisis bloom worked in this lab. In some jurisdictions around the country, officers can use field kits to test powders and pills on location, but not here. When unidentified substances arrive at Baltimore police headquarters—brought in by officers, detectives, or the crime scene team, they usually get sorted into the drug unit. Generally speaking, this is how it works across the department: suspected biological clues go to bio, guns go to firearms, and anything that might be a controlled substance—e.g., fentanyl—comes here.*

When strange liquids or powders arrive in the drug lab, analysts remove small samples and place them inside GC-MS (gas chromatography-mass spectrometry) machines. GC-MS is a versatile, all-purpose chemical analysis technique used in

---

* Some pieces of evidence do move through more than one unit, such as a gun that needs to be screened for latent fingerprints. This is pretty rare for drugs, though. "Occasionally, somebody will ask us to swab a drug bag for DNA," DellaRocco says. "But usually it's like, *We want to know what this substance is because we took it off of 'Paul.' It doesn't really matter if his DNA is on it, because we took it out of his pocket.*"

industries as diverse as environmental monitoring, medicine development, and fragrance creation. It splits compounds into their constituent parts, like a prism fracturing light into a rainbow, then assigns each part a molecular signature. Analysts compare the signatures created by unknown samples to those created by pure samples, purchased from vetted labs. If the signatures match, then you know what you've got.

Supervisors in Baltimore's drug lab choose a slate of control samples to run every week, based on a changing list of what has been appearing in the department. Cocaine, heroin, and delta-9-tetrahydrocannabinol (THC, the psychoactive chemical in marijuana) are regulars. Drugs that materialize less frequently, such as 3,4-methylenedioxymethamphetamine (MDMA, or "molly"), hydrocodone (Vicodin, for example), and methylphenidate (Ritalin), get run as one-offs, whenever necessary.

Around 2015, supervisors in the drug chemistry lab noticed they needed standards of fentanyl more and more often. Previously, fentanyl identifications had spiked and dissipated, spiked and dissipated. This time, they steadily increased. By the end of 2015, the supervisors had to add a second fentanyl-based standard to the weekly list, a mix of fentanyl and tramadol, another opioid. They added furanyl fentanyl, a designer analog, to the list in 2017. In March of 2018, fentanyl identifications surpassed heroin to become the third most identified substance in the entire lab, right behind marijuana and cocaine. It was a crisis, and Baltimore's drug lab was on the front lines. Johns Hopkins University called: Could they partner up to validate fentanyl testing strips for harm reduction?

Fentanyl is an extreme case, but drug chemistry units are always trailing one step behind the public, uncovering drug trends as they happen in real time. This can, obviously, be a very dangerous position to be in. Techs are as careful as they can be, but they're not working in a CDC-caliber negative pressure room. It's just a regular lab, where exotic mystery substances that could be anything pass through like breezes.

Procedures had long been in place to prevent any of the analysts from becoming accidentally intoxicated. Analysts wear gloves and open large batches under fume hoods. After fentanyl, the lab bought up twenty-six doses of NARCAN and stashed them all over the place, including on the cart that ferries packages back and forth to evidence control. Analysts started wearing face masks more often. A command came down from the brass for everyone to ditch their personal desk fans so that if there were any errant grains, they wouldn't get blown around.

The wet lab is the most worrisome because it's where analysts perform physical evaluations: weighing the samples and removing just enough of a substance to run it through GC-MS. Sometimes the analysts in this room perform preliminary tests, called color tests, that can slot drugs into categories, although they've been phasing those out. Color tests increase chemists' exposure to the drugs and aren't as streamlined as other options.

The second room, where the GC-MS machines chug along doing their robot stuff, is safer. These tests require very small amounts of pills and powders, and what there is remains sealed within airtight machinery. DellaRocco and I walk through this room to reach the sunny office of Rachel Lucas, another high-achieving woman who was, at the time, the drug lab's technical lead.*

According to Lucas, the most substantial difference between the drug unit and the rest of the forensic labs is

---

* Since the publication of this book, Lucas has left the Baltimore city police department for a new position with the county (amicably, and not because of the fentanyl).

that a gumshoe wouldn't have much use for what they do in here. While the drug lab can advise task forces on undercover buys and requirements for prosecution, it rarely helps locate the overseer of an international fentanyl lab the way the fingerprint lab points a detective to a murderer. Mostly, chemical reports get deployed in court to answer the second statement of an argument in formal logic:

> Statement 1: If these are drugs, then the state is
> going to punish you.
>
> Statement 2: Are these drugs?

For this reason, the supervisors stay in close touch with various FBI and state's attorney's task forces, finding out when cases are going to court, and which statutes—local, state, or federal—need to be considered with regard to amounts and types. Prioritization is key. With samples coming in like rain, Lucas doesn't want to waste her analysts on cases that will never see a judge.

Lucas stays in *such* close touch with the state's attorney's office that when she realized the nested *whereas*-es of a new agricultural bill were going to cause a disaster for her unit, she was the one to call *them*. The bill was Maryland's House Bill 1123, Chapter 228—intended to promote hemp as a commodity. People were calling it the "farm bill."

Both Lucas and DellaRocco start laughing incredulously when they talk about this legal boondoggle. I'm sure you'll be surprised to hear this, but politicians don't necessarily have any scientific background, so sometimes they enact laws that don't make sense. The farm bill was supposed to allow production of hemp-based products that furthered agricultural research, but only if "hemp" meant cannabis products that contained less than 0.3 percent of the plant's psychoactive chemical, THC. Defining hemp in terms of THC content was not so crazy—previous federal bills had done the same for similar reasons. The problem was that in Maryland recreational marijuana remained illegal: logically, if any cannabis product that contained less than 0.3 percent THC was hemp, then only those products that contained *more* than 0.3 percent THC were against the law.

It had somehow occurred to no one in the Maryland house, senate, or governor's office that forensic drug labs were not accredited to quantify THC. When Lucas personally called and informed the state's attorney's office that the new hemp law would put them in a logical bind, the state's attorney's office was nonplussed. *Why would we care about the farm bill?* they said.

Lucas laughs—a real can-you-believe-this-shit guffaw. If you don't have a court-admissible test for THC purity, then you can't officially differentiate between hemp (legal) and marijuana (illegal). Even if a fat, crystal-covered nugget shows up on the evidence cart with the word MARIJUANA stamped on it in block letters, the lab can't, legally, tell a jury it is marijuana.

To solve this problem, DellaRocco, alongside the staff of the drug lab, asked for and received funding for a new machine, a ridiculously sensitive chemical analyzer called a Triple Quad LC (or, more formally, a liquid chromatography triple quadrupole mass spectrometer). This machine *can* perform quantitative measurements of THC, but before the lab can use it, they've got to validate it. That means the technical lead will research the triple quad's stats and capabilities, the ways other labs use it, and any information on the chemistry or procedures involved. The lead will propose tests, including any requirements from the state or from the FBI, or from the lab's various accreditation bodies. Then the technical lead will perform those tests. "Between the time to purchase it and the time to get it installed and then the time to validate it, it'll probably be another year [before we can use the triple quad]," DellaRocco says.

In the meantime, all marijuana evaluations for every forensic lab in the state of Maryland are on hold. And whether you think that's a positive development from a drug policy perspective or not, it's certainly inefficient.

A QUESTION PEOPLE OFTEN ask around the drug lab is what happens to all the drugs after they've been analyzed? Who disposes of them, and where? The answer is that both the evidence control unit and the drug chemistry unit stage regular drug elimination burns. Each time, the internal affairs office inspects the contraband and the staff loads it into an unmarked white box truck. A caravan proceeds to an incinerator in the following order: one lead car, one armored truck, unmarked box truck full of drugs, van containing the staff who will do the unloading, then a tailing unmarked police car. There is no stopping on the way to the incinerator, no matter what.

The staff who run the drug burns have offered to let Rachel Lucas attend one, which she admits sounds super cool. However, she once saw a TV episode, she thinks it was *NYPD Blue*, in which criminals attempted to rob a drug burn caravan. By the end of the episode, absolutely everybody had been murdered. "Sounds great, but no thank you," she always says.

7

FINGERPRINTS

It is incredible that fingerprints even exist, that shallow labyrinths more unique than human faces form on the surfaces of the body most likely to touch things. Look down at your fingertips, at the curves and convolutions. Everything you're looking at is backward. If you left a print on something it would appear in reverse, as if you were looking out at the world from the center of your finger.

What does your fingerprint look like? Concentric ridges arranged into arches, whorls, or loops? Click on your cell phone's flashlight. Look again. In the center of my left middle finger is a tiny triskelion made up of three loops, a yin and yang in triplicate. Below that, two ridges bifurcate to enclose a dead ringer for that little island in the middle of Paris. How have I never noticed that the pad of my thumb looks like a river delta? What the heck is going on?

That people have unique fingerprints at all is an accident.

At ten to twelve weeks of development, the outer layer of a fetus's see-through skin begins forming light corrugations that halt, split, and pull away from one another as the fingers first shrink and then expand in size. Like wind creating waves far out at sea, the random inputs complicate into patterns as environmental variables bear down on all sides. The ridges form the same way rain streaks across a car windshield during a rainstorm. The droplets halt and split and slam into each other as they dash across the glass.

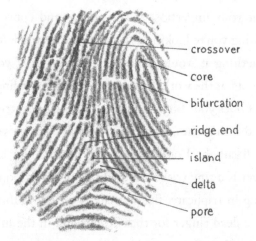

crossover

core

bifurcation

ridge end

island

delta

pore

The point here is that fingerprints are physical manifestations of the chaos of development, unique even among twins. For nearly a century before DNA technology was invented in the 1980s, they were the least-biased method for identifying an individual. Now, with DNA and computer face and voice and iris identification and other postmodern technologies, you could be forgiven for wondering what role they play in crime-solving. Do we still need fingerprints?

In short, yes. A detective's job is to build a case strong enough to convict a criminal. A crime lab is simply a tool he can use, same as a medical lab. If additional tests can be performed cheaply, quickly, and decisively, the way fingerprint analysis can, detectives tend to be maximalists about them. The more elements that can be brought to bear on a case, the better.

Of course, that's assuming you've got someone who knows how to match fingerprints, which is harder than it sounds.

SYLVIA BUFFINGTON-LESTER HAS ONE of those sweet tea, pecan pie southern accents, thick as pimento dip. In sixteen years at the FBI and a little more than thirty years at the Virginia Department of Forensic Science in Richmond, she has spent a long time in the South. She was also, before she retired, one of the foremost experts on fingerprint analysis in the country. Now, at seventy, she has pulled back, teaching adjunct classes in forensic science at Virginia Commonwealth University and performing occasional shows as a jazz singer. Listening to her pronounce the word "blouse," in two and a half syllables, I imagine she's fantastic.

The Virginia Department of Forensic Science is a little different from Baltimore's in-house forensic laboratory unit. Analysts here process fingerprints—or more properly, friction skin markings, including palm and bare footprints—from start to finish. During Buffington-Lester's tenure, she did it all: the science stuff, including exposing hidden prints with cyanoacrylate; the gross stuff, which sometimes involved removing skin from the hands of dead bodies; and the art.

If your only experiences with fingerprint analysis are TV shows, where examiners scan found prints into a database that immediately brings up the image of the person who committed the crime, it may not be clear what artistry is involved in the process. Scan print. Get hit. Go home. But this is not how fingerprint analysis works. It usually takes eighteen months of training to learn how to do it. There is a database, the Automated Fingerprint Identification System, or AFIS, but it functions more like a suggestion engine. If an analyst doesn't have a suspect to compare a found print to, she can upload what she's got and get back a list of candidate prints. She has to make all further decisions—the serious, someone-is-going-to-jail decisions—using her eyes.

Determining how two fingerprints relate to each other, whether their stable, developmentally produced characteristics are identical, is a feat of visual acuity on par with recognizing cancer in radiographic images. While, in theory, anyone can learn to do it, it is much easier for those who have "the eye." Buffington-Lester can tell when one of her students has the eye. Some of them can look at a fingerprint and naturally cleave the whorls from the arches from the loops, can perceive the smaller forms intuitively, the way an artist breaks a figure into panes of light. She has it herself, an artistic sense of the world that helps her see what others don't. "I could buy a chartreuse blouse, and two years later see something that's that same shade of green, and buy it," she says. "And sure enough, when I get it home it will match."

On one case Buffington-Lester worked in the early '90s, a roll of cash register tape came in for processing from a store that had experienced a number of internal thefts. The owner suspected that the thief was tearing out the transactions during which he or she had taken money, then taping the pre- and post-sections of the receipt scroll together, rolling the whole thing up, and turning it in at the end of the day. The owner delivered the rolls in their entirety to the local police department for processing. The police department sent them to the Virginia Department of Forensic Science.

Because receipt tape is porous, Buffington-Lester treated it with a chemical called ninhydrin, one of those dozen-or-so techniques that can expose latent fingerprints on evidence. Little purple prints appeared all over the place. Strangely, there appeared to be two sets: one on the paper itself, and a second set underneath the tape. With modern computer systems, Buffington-Lester could have uploaded the prints, moved them around, or attempted to flip or stack them to see what was going on. Back then, all she had was a magnifier.

Leaning over the unrolled receipt paper, Buffington-Lester felt like there was something uncanny about the prints on the tape. They were different, but they also weren't. She looked at the splits, the bends, the broken pieces. Then it hit her. The set of prints on the tape were on the sticky side, in mirror image. Thank God for her eye—she pulled over the set of suspect's known prints, and went ahead and compared half of them backward.

IN A CONFERENCE ROOM in the Baltimore Police Department, Sean Dorr draws a fingerprint on a sheet of my notebook paper, a series of parallel arches with splits and spurs heading off them. "There are three basic types of friction ridge details," he says. Dots are directionless units that appear as a blip on the lift card. Ending ridges flow until they come to an abrupt stop at something else. Bifurcations are just what they sound like: ridges that split into two or more pieces.

These details are what analysts are comparing when they look at fingerprints—not necessarily whether you've got whorls or arches or loops, which are just general categories, but whether the spatial arrangement of the peculiar minutiae in two prints cannot be explained by anything but sameness. Fingerprints from crime scenes don't come in neat and orderly, after all. They arrive in several ways: as photographs from scenes; as photographs from the forensic bio unit; or, more often, on lift cards. The mobile unit produces the lift cards on scene, using a brush to swirl powders* over hard surfaces, pressing clear tape on top, and attaching the lifted print to a card to preserve it in perpetuity. Under any of these circumstances, the prints might arrive smeared, skewed, or in pieces. You may only have a few ridges to focus on, and in that case you've got to hope you can find enough quirky patterns to reach a quorum.

Friction skin analysts perform their intricate work under quiet, library-like conditions: Next to a shelf of favorite reference books, say. Under a particular lamp. Dorr uses a five-dollar, adjustable-neck LED lamp from Target that he angles at precisely 30 degrees so the light hits the prints from the side. He slides the prints, on cardstock, under a pair of 5x magnifiers with spindly legs so that light can pass through underneath. Five times is about as high as he'll go on magnification: any more and the distortion and background noise gets overwhelming.

Dorr compares fingerprints the same way you'd sink into a lake. First, he determines what he's looking at—a

---

* Fingerprint powders usually come in black, colored, or magnetic varieties. Back when she worked scenes, Rana DellaRocco preferred magnetic. It's less messy than plain black because the technician applies it using a magnetic wand, which the powder sticks to like a buzzcut. When swirled over a non-porous surface, magnetic powder sticks to the oils in fingerprints, but otherwise doesn't get all over victims' houses.

finger? A palm? He orients the print—left hand, right hand, up, down. Slots it into a category of arch, whorl, or loop. Then he slides lower to observe the details, keeping track of them with a little metal pointer. One specific feature, or a grouping of them. His favorites are combinations, when dots, ending ridges, or bifurcations occur next to or on top of each other. Take the little Parisian island on my middle finger. That's an enclosure, two bifurcations aimed at each other like this [lt][gt]. A great place to start.

From the initial feature or group, Dorr moves out like a ripple, finding, grabbing, and adding other details to establish an overall pattern. There might be a hundred features in a print, the majority of them ending ridges. The second you find something in one print that doesn't appear in the other, you exclude that person from having committed the crime. But if it keeps matching and matching, at some point you've got to make a decision: Do you have enough? Is this the guy?

In fingerprints, as in most analysis labs, a second pair of eyes always confirms what the first analyst sees, to prevent any false matches. It's very easy to second-guess yourself—especially in situations where there's high background noise. Prints on money are the worst, with all those squiggles and lines behind the ridges. "Anything fluorescent, if you look at that too long, you almost want your eyes to melt out of your head," Dorr says. He's marched down to the field office and told them to stop buying that pink powder they'd been using to dust for prints at crime scenes. He doesn't like the green, either. What's wrong with plain black?

The more complicated a print is, the more likely Dorr is to imagine a sheet of graph paper behind it, sectioning any details into quadrants to keep them straight. He learned this trick in mechanical drawing classes, which he took when he studied engineering in college. "Then I realized I hate math," he says.

Dorr originally wanted to be a "DNA cop" as he used to think of it after watching *Matlock* and *Manhunter*. But he wasn't as lucky as Rana DellaRocco in terms of timing. When Dorr joined Baltimore PD in 1999, they still didn't have their own DNA lab. After less than a year in the mobile unit, he got volunteered ("volun-told," some techs say) to do the scientific processing of prints—the ninhydrin, cyanoacrylate resurfacing stuff—in the latent print lab. Eventually, Dorr's supervisor asked him if he might want to give comparing the prints a shot too. In the way that people's careers can suddenly switch tracks and trundle off toward new destinations, there it was: Dorr became a fingerprint analyst.

"Now I'm like DNA what?" he says. He loves prints: In his opinion, they are the most simple, prescriptive science in forensic science. Unlike shoe prints or swipings of car paint, they give you a unique person. You can't contaminate them, like you can with DNA. There are no unusual situations in which two prints might accidentally be the same for some crazy science fiction reason. One print is one person—not a set of twins or someone with chimerism (two or more complete sets of genes within a single body. Look it up, it's wild), or anything else unexpected.

But even in this lab, things change. Over the last ten years, computers have profoundly altered the landscape of fingerprint analysis. As of late 2019, the analysts can compare prints in Photoshop, darkening or lightening an image or changing it to grayscale to correct for heavy powdering or a colorful background. Dorr says he should like this. He loves computers, is a serious Star Wars fan, down to the huge, impressively detailed tattoos of twin lightsaber hilts that race down his forearms. It's just that he trained for so long comparing prints by hand that it doesn't feel right to look at them in pixels. He still takes a run at new prints on paper cards under his magnifier before displaying them up on his dual-screen monitor.

Lately, more and more fingerprint analysts have begun using Photoshop layers to mark off telling details as they find them. The system they use to do this is called GYRO, an acronym for green-yellow-red-orange. As an analyst finds details that classify a print, he annotates an image with different colored dots based on how confident he is in the details' presence. Green is for highly confident. Red is for highly uncertain. Yellow is for in-between. Orange is for details an analyst only noticed after taking a look at a clearer, cleaner comparison print, such as those a police officer took from a suspect at a station.

The spread of GYRO may mean that fingerprint analysts end up testifying in court less often. After Dorr has completed a print comparison, he burns his Photoshop file onto a CD that is delivered to the lawyers working a case. In court, the lawyer can load that up and show a jury exactly how Dorr came to his conclusion without needing to have him there to explain it. "I'm not sad about that at all," Dorr says. It's not that he hates going to court. He just hates waiting for hours up on the benches when he could be back at his desk working cases.

GYRO is a solid step forward for objective jurisprudence, but the same way the shift to computers has discomfited fingerprint analysts, formally labeling confidence has also been an uncomfortable change. When you've been using a sense of intuition to guide your eye for more than fifteen years, and suddenly your boss is asking you to spell out why you know what you know in color-coded layers of confidence, of course it's going to slow you down.

Dorr has been a certified print examiner for sixteen years. He's looked at hundreds of thousands of friction skin markings. He doesn't have to mentally check boxes to see the patterns anymore. When the previous technical lead recently left Baltimore's fingerprint department, Dorr inherited five trainees to see through to certification. He thinks they're great and smart and can't wait to see them stand on their own, but sometimes one of them will be analyzing a sample print and will have it oriented incorrectly on his desk. It takes all of Dorr's self-control not to just walk over, spin the sheet and say, *It goes this way.*

Sometimes in the evening, Dorr will come home from work, switch on the local news and catch the anchors talking about a crime. A little graphic of a fingerprint will pop up in the corner. Just a little nod to Sherlock Holmes to liven up the broadcast.

It drives Dorr nuts, of course. "It's upside down," he moans.

8

GUNS

At nine thirty a.m. on December 14, 2017, two days of random terror began at a food market in northwest Baltimore. A man opened fire from the window of a silver sedan, striking a victim in the upper arm. Five hours later, what looked like the same silver sedan halted in the middle of St. Ambrose Avenue, just a few blocks away. A handgun appeared in the driver's-side window and shot Martell Harris in the head and the neck as he crossed the street. Harris died at a nearby hospital.

At 4:50 p.m., according to video footage, a silver sedan pulled up in front of a store on Poplar Grove Street, three miles south of the other two attacks. This time, an assault-style rifle snaked out of the driver's-side window, peppering the store with bullets. At least one projectile blasted through a wall and killed Ali Ouedraogo, a clerk, while he was performing his evening prayers.

As always, Baltimore's crime scene unit began searching

for clues. At the food market, technicians found six .40-caliber cartridge cases and one bullet lying on the ground. Near St. Ambrose Avenue, they found five more cartridge cases, also .40 caliber. The third location was littered with 7.62 x 39mm cases, typical of those used in assault rifles. As a lead, it wasn't much to go on. A better option was the silver sedan. It matched the description of a car involved in another random shooting, what seemed like a road rage incident involving a minivan, all the way back on December 8.

The following day, police stopped a silver, four-door 2005 Lexus at a roadblock. The driver, Mausean Carter, initially cooperated, but then fired at officers and sped off, leading the police on a fifty-minute car chase through West Baltimore. While the cops pursued him, Carter fired indiscriminately at people in cars and on the street. He injured three people, one critically. Eventually, Carter's girlfriend sprinted across a five-lane road while he continued shooting, dragged him out of the car, and covered him with her body. Baltimore's chief of media relations would praise her on television, saying, "She put herself in the middle of harm's way" to help.

Even as Carter confessed, Baltimore's firearms lab swung into action. The shootings had all taken place from the driver's seat of a car, which didn't leave much likelihood of finding fingerprints or DNA evidence on or near the victims. The goal: link six or seven crime scenes to each other, and back to the 7.62 x 39mm semiautomatic rifle and .40-caliber Smith & Wesson pistol found in Carter's car, using nothing but cartridge cases and bullets.

FIREARMS ANALYSIS IS AN old practice. Older than DNA, older than fingerprinting, older even than crime scene investigation as a discipline. Although Calvin Goddard popularized the science in the U.S. in the 1930s, its first recorded use was in 1835. A member of an early London police force called the Bow Street Runners connected a lead ball and a wad of newsprint used in a murder to a ballistics mold and a matching ripped newspaper found in the perpetrator's room.

Conceptually, connecting spent ammunition to a firearm is simple: A firearm is a human-made machine—hard, imperfect, and potentially unique. The marks it imparts on softer metals, such as brass cartridges and lead bullets, ought to lead an investigator straight back to it. Doing this in practice, however, requires a colossal accumulation of knowledge. "You can't memorize all of it; there are millions and millions of guns out there," says Jennifer Ingbretson, an eighteen-year veteran of Baltimore's forensics team with seven years in the firearms lab.

Baltimore's firearm reference library alone houses 2,500 samples, including rifles; revolvers; shotguns and pistols; guns inside canes; guns inside pens; a Raging Bull revolver that can take down a wild boar in one shot; high-powered assault rifles of the kind commonly used in mass shootings; a whole rack of firearms so small a woman could hide them in her palm; and a *rocket launcher*. The library, a space no larger than an apartment bedroom, looks like one of those spy-movie weapon closets, although any would-be Kingsman who outfitted himself in here would come out looking like a postapocalyptic marauder, carrying a mismatched arsenal of Tommy guns and pocket pistols.

Ingbretson jokes that the gun library exists mostly to entertain visitors like me, but it's also a convenient place for newbies to get a handle on just how different the different parts of weapons can be, and how that might affect their daily work. Most modern guns fire self-contained ammunition, which means a cartridge stuffed with a propellant (gunpowder, for example), a bullet or shot, and a small shock-sensitive explosive charge called a primer. To shoot a bullet, an average semiautomatic pistol must detonate the primer so that it ignites the propellant, spin the bullet on its way down the barrel (for accuracy), and eject the spent cartridge case to replace it with a new cartridge.

Any of the unyielding metal bits involved in these processes can mark bullets and/or cartridge cases, but in practice, four do the majority of the damage: the *firing pin* punches the cartridge when it detonates the primer; the cartridge recoils against the gun's *breech face* as the propellant ignites and builds gas; *lands* (raised surfaces) of a barrel's spiral rifling scar the bullet as they spin it out toward its target, and *ejector and extractor* mechanisms leave bands and grooves as they expel spent cases from the gun.

The shapes and sizes of these four parts in various gun models create predictable patterns of markings called "class characteristics": When a cartridge explodes backward upon igniting in a Beretta, for example, the weapon's breech face imprints little arcs in the back of the casing. Under the same circumstances, Glocks and S&W Sigma series firearms create parallel lines. If you see either mark on a piece of evidence, and you know what you're looking at, you can narrow your search for a corresponding weapon.

Of course, it gets more complicated. Within classes you'll find "subclass characteristics," factory changes, malfunctions, or events that create subsets of makes and models. A manufacturer's cutting machine with a chunk missing might build a whole batch of guns with a screwy groove in the rifling, for example. And then, beneath that, individual firearms differ in noticeable ways. This is what makes the identification of a single firearm from a piece of ballistics evidence possible. While some justice advocates question whether the markings a firearm creates are fully unique among all those in the world, a gun's position on the assembly line, random imperfections in machining of its parts, how many times it was fired, how it was maintained, and where it was stored create telltale impressions that most police agencies believe can connect it to a single spent cartridge or bullet. The only way to become proficient enough in markings to make such connections is the same way a fisherman learns the ocean: observe, observe, observe.

Jennifer Ingbretson is uniquely qualified to explain how much work it takes to become proficient in firearms analysis, because she spent most of her career doing something else. Prior to taking her current position, she worked in Baltimore's DNA lab for twelve years, ever since arriving on contractual loan from an immigration and paternity lab. Around 2014, she grew restless. She'd been doing the same thing her entire career. All of her continuing education had been in the DNA and biology arena. She started to wonder if she should work toward a second master's degree, or a PhD, to keep herself sharp.

Allowing analysts to transition between specialties is a characteristic shared by some of the top forensic labs in the country. It forestalls some of the hazards inherent in employing a population of extremely smart and curious people. In a department that allows it, an easily bored analyst can have several fundamentally different careers while continuing to work for the same employer, preventing boredom, burnout, brain drain, and attrition.

At first, it was humbling for Ingbretson to return to the bottom of the knowledge hierarchy. She'd known everything there was to know about DNA, but firearms was an

entirely different world. It takes a solid three years to become certified in this lab, beginning with six months of
reading old books.* After that, you have to learn to inven-
tory guns, take them apart and put them back together, and,
eventually, put in hours and hours of "scope time," to develop the acuity necessary to compare markings on bullets
and spent cartridges.

The culture of the firearms lab was also alien to someone coming from DNA. The rooms themselves are louder
and more boisterous. The analysts dress less formally. According to Ingbretson, firearms examiners tend to come to
work in jeans and keep their good court clothes in their
lockers. Instead of relying on high-tech machines and
swooping in at the end to perform brain-melting statistics
like she did in DNA, Ingbretson now works with her hands
constantly. She is adjusting a microscope; flicking through
an old wooden library card catalog filled with disassembled
ammo; taking potshots at an indoor waterfall.

Did I mention the indoor waterfall? It's part of a minia-

---

* Such as, for example, *Hatcher's Notebook*, a primer on gun makers, gun
varieties, gun parts, and gun functions, as well as ballistics, ammunition, ranges,
weights, and any number of other ephemera. It was written by army major
general and ordnance expert Julian Hatcher in 1947 and remains surprisingly
relevant today.

ture gun range analysts use to test-fire suspicious weapons. Formally called a snail trap, it sends a sludge of oil and water cascading down a slanted surface to prevent bullets from ricocheting all over a shooting studio the size of a bathroom. Analysts use the snail trap when they need to produce and collect spent cartridges for comparisons. If they need the bullets themselves, they shoot into a water tank one room over.

One other thing a firearms examiner has to master before she can be considered an expert is another database. While the DNA lab loads its finds into CODIS and the fingerprint lab retrieves potential matches from AFIS, firearms examiners are serfs laboring at the pleasure of the National Integrated Ballistic Information Network (NIBIN), maintained by the United States Bureau of Alcohol, Tobacco, Firearms and Explosives (ATF). And sometimes, especially lately, the database really feels like a demanding feudal lord.

NIBIN is a series of interlinked terminals in firearms labs all over the country. It came into use in the early 2000s with the goal of establishing connections among firearms discharges to help police link crimes and track criminals. In an ideal world, every jurisdiction would upload images of cartridge cases (NIBIN also accommodates images of bullets, but Baltimore doesn't contribute them) to their own terminal, for every incident, no matter how low-priority. Algorithms would flag similarities between cartridges quickly, and an expert would confirm them while the criminals were still at large. Police would use NIBIN's leads to catch gun-using criminals before they escalated to more serious violence.

Only, as of the mid-2010s, this was not exactly happening. Few police departments had the manpower, or the interest, to input every single piece of ballistics evidence that came through their doors into the system. A National Institute of Justice report released in 2013 called the program underfunded. The authors found that some jurisdictions weren't inputting enough of their ballistics evidence into NIBIN, that they weren't doing it quickly enough, or that they weren't communicating what they found with police who could act on it.

One of the report's suggestions was to dispense with requiring "hits" to guide law enforcement actions, and instead use a slightly less rigorous standard. To get a hit, analysts had to upload images of cartridge cases that the network would use to find a potential match, then acquire and compare the physical cartridge cases in person, which could take weeks if the pieces were located in different places. By the time the finalized hits were up and available, the police had often already solved the case, or the trail had gone cold. As the report authors (dryly) put it: "During a visit to a major U.S. police agency . . . when homicide investigators were asked about the use of ballistic evidence, they laughed and said the lab takes so long to provide results that they don't even bother asking anymore."

Sobered by the report and bolstered with $26 million in new funding in the wake of the Newtown, Connecticut, massacre, ATF encouraged analysts to focus on "leads" as an alternative to hits. Leads were, essentially, algorithmic links that had been seen by an analyst, but hadn't been confirmed under a microscope. These, ATF said, could guide detectives on their investigations before being formally corroborated for court. ATF also decreed that, by December 31, 2020, leads needed to be uploaded within two business days (forty-eight hours) of a gun or ballistics evidence arriving in an evidence unit. There would be no shirking this requirement: They'd be coming around doing audits.

At first, Baltimore's analysts chafed at the new restrictions. Several thousand cartridge cases moved through the firearms lab every year. Tight time constraints were a big ask. And what was the point of performing rigorous analyses if you were just going to put your unproven thoughts out in public before completing them? "It goes against everything you typically hear in accreditation; you don't release preliminary information: never, never, never," Rana DellaRocco says. "So all of us were like . . . *eek*."

Still, in the service of being useful (and also because ATF said they had to) the lab stepped up. By March of 2020, the firearms unit had attained an on-time rate of 94.2 percent under the new 48-hour restriction, putting them at number 13 out of 230 listed NIBIN sites in the country, ahead of such jurisdictions as New York City, Chicago, and Los Angeles. They had to admit: even if it was tough, the new rule moved the lab in a positive direction. Crime scene analysts always want detectives to use their skills more to prevent crime, rather than less. Take the Mausean Carter case: if the lab could quickly provide a NIBIN match to guide police alongside what they already knew about the silver sedan, they would want to provide it.

In the microscope room, someone has taped half a sheet of paper to the bottom of the NIBIN terminal. It's a picture of the villain Jigsaw from the horror movie series *Saw*, about a murderer who traps his victims in nightmarish predicaments and provides them a limited window of time to escape.

"You have forty-eight hours," the picture says. "The clock is ticking."

9

THE CHIEF

It was the day before the night before Christmas, and people were finally leaving Chief Steven O'Dell alone. Downstairs in the Bishop L. Robinson Sr. Police Administration Building, just three people waited by the front desk. "You have a Merry Christmas!" echoed an officer's goodbye as he walked out the door.

Upstairs, tinsel trees huddled in the corners of the hallways. Windows into many of the labs were dark. The operation wasn't on hold—the labs work on business hours, but they never really close, and the mobile unit stays open 365 days a year. But forensic science, like many sciences, attracts early risers. Everyone who had gotten started at seven a.m. and had managed to secure a day or two off was already on their way home.

O'Dell, who heads up Baltimore's entire forensics operation, stands when I walk into his office. He's been back from Iraq for seven years, but hasn't lost the ramrod posture, or the unsettling habit of rarely breaking eye contact. Or maybe he was always like that. O'Dell has two bachelor's degrees, two master's degrees, two certifications from the American Board of Criminalistics, once passed a top-secret security clearance, and is working on two doctorates and a couple of associate's degrees. For fun. He's an intense guy.

Anyway, I'd tell you what's on the chief's desk, which is actually two desks arranged into an L-shape against the wall, neither fancy like *The Wire* nor cigarette-burned like also *The Wire*, but I couldn't get my pupils to myself long enough to peek at it. What I can tell you for sure is that O'Dell's eyes are as blue as stonewashed denim. There's gray in his goatee. His name tag is an aggressively informal piece of folded paper from a former police commissioner's first COMSTAT (crime strategy update) meeting, in which the commissioner had provided handwritten name tags for "all the important people at the table." The commissioner, whom O'Dell doesn't name but who seems somewhat obviously to be Darryl De Sousa, was later sentenced to ten months in federal prison for failing to file tax returns. O'Dell kept the name tag as a little inside joke.

In case it's not clear from that little anecdote, Chief O'Dell has lived a life so interesting that he can't (or at least won't) tell people about parts of it. In the beginning, he grew up in the Vermont mountain town of St. Albans, just twelve miles from the Canadian border. He shoveled snow and chopped wood, skied, and ice-skated, but never got so sentimental about rural New England that he wasn't willing to follow his high school girlfriend, a cheerleader, to Arizona State University. Arizona was the opposite of Vermont, the weather reliable and unchanging. The glass in the modern buildings was always shining in the sunlight. O'Dell loved it.

Another student blind to the possibilities of forensics because crime scene shows were not yet on television, O'Dell chose his twin majors at Arizona State not because he hoped to connect them but because he saw in each a potential future. If he went the justice studies route, he could be a cop. Microbiology would set him on the path to medical school. Unsure which it would be, he must have changed his major five times: pre-med, pre-law, business, back and forth. By the end, he had accumulated more than two hundred credits.

In 1999, the fall of their senior year, O'Dell's new girlfriend started scouring the country for doctorate programs in microbiology. (Like the majority of high school sweethearts who go off to college together, he and the cheerleader had broken up soon after matriculation.) Over dial-up modem, O'Dell started looking for his next step as well. He typed "science and police" into an AOL search engine, and criminalistics came up, along with one of the few master's programs then available, at the University of Alabama at Birmingham. O'Dell's new girlfriend was admitted to the excellent cellular and molecular biology program at the same school. They moved to the deep South.

Like DellaRocco, O'Dell is relentless in his pursuit of

classes, qualifications, degrees, and training. At UAB, he won a graduate assistantship that allowed him to work at the Alabama Department of Forensic Sciences (ADFS), processing samples for CODIS while he completed his degree. Because the ADFS also functioned as the state medical examiner's office, it also offered pathology technician training in the morgue. A crime scene investigator didn't even need that, but O'Dell did it anyway.

After graduation, O'Dell stayed on at the AFDS, taking a track in which employees could become sworn police officers. In addition to doing casework on location and screening bodily fluids and DNA (this was during one of those periods when CSIs were still somewhat generalists), O'Dell picked up legal knowledge at the state law enforcement academy and set himself on a quicker path to a pension. In a few years, he became an exceptionally well-rounded forensic scientist, even by modern standards. Back then, there were few like him. Still, he was making just $27,000 a year. When his girlfriend, who had taken a job as a lab scientist at the Veterans Administration, suggested transferring to a job back in Arizona, O'Dell happily agreed.

The commander of the Phoenix Police Department's forensic bureau was also a sworn officer, same as O'Dell. They hit it off immediately. DNA analysis was spreading fast, and O'Dell got involved in reorganizing the department. When the National Forensic Science and Technology Center asked O'Dell to write a module for the George W. Bush–era President's DNA Initiative, a government call to develop DNA programs at police departments, his boss allowed him to work on it. O'Dell began traveling around the country training other analysts. And that's the end of the part of O'Dell's life that he'll talk about without intermittently squinting at your tape recorder and giving you a look like he's assessing whether he'll have to kill you when this is all over.

The forensic community in this country is tiny, under twenty thousand people all told. Everyone knows each other—now, but even more so back then. O'Dell is pretty confident the defense contractor found him through his work on the President's Initiative and periodic excursions to other departments. The company, Ideal Innovations, reached out over LinkedIn. The Iraq war had begun, and they were launching deployable laboratories in the Middle East called JEFFs (Joint Expeditionary Forensics Facilities) that would help the military identify insurgents using DNA. Would he want to help with something like that?

O'Dell was fairly content in Phoenix—the sunlight! The

modern buildings!—and said no. But a few years later his personal life was on the rocks. The contractor got in touch again, asking for help with a more enticing program, training Iraqi police to use objective evidence in their own criminal proceedings, plus something-something military intelligence. "Like every good man, I ran away from my problems," O'Dell says. This time, O'Dell said yes.

O'Dell went overseas, initially with Ideal Innovations, but he got picked up by another contractor called Dyncorp, and, eventually, the Department of State. Details on exactly *what* he did for the Department of State are thin. But he was in-community, stationed in villages and working directly with Iraqi police. It stands to reason that, while helping to investigate crimes, he kept an ear to the ground for any information that might be of interest to certain people.

At one point, alone in a de facto shipping container outside Baghdad and far from anyone who could help ("We called them 'cans,'" he says), O'Dell had a heart attack. He knew it was a heart attack because angina had been stabbing him in the left shoulder for months. Sometimes bending over and putting his arm over his head helped. In the can, in the middle of the night, he tried that. He hunched over his desk, trying to breathe. This time the position didn't help. The pain continued for thirty seconds. Sixty seconds. Ninety. This one might really be it, he thought.

As a lifelong crime scene investigator might, O'Dell immediately thought about how he'd be found. He had seen bodies in positions like the one he was in—knew that out here, no one would think to look for him for weeks. It would probably be one of his coworkers that would find him, and he would be bloated, messy, and stinking. Naked. To say that that outcome was unpalatable was putting it mildly.

Seconds lasted hours. O'Dell tried to breathe. He didn't want to go home. His success making it all the way out here felt like a force that demanded continuance. He gathered up as much stubbornness as he could and decided he was not going to have a heart attack in a shipping container in Iraq. And so he didn't. Or, he did, but he didn't die. The pain went away. And that was that.

How O'Dell ended up here in Baltimore is another interesting story. To send money anywhere from Iraq, he and his buddies used to have to go to the village Western Union, where the clerk was a local woman with beautiful hair named Lina. O'Dell saw Lina just once and thought she was cute, but didn't have the guts to ask her out.

The second time O'Dell saw Lina, she asked him for his

phone number. You had to provide it if you were going to receive or send money. Pretty standard anywhere. Only, with all the switching out of SIM cards he was doing, O'Dell couldn't remember what his phone number was. Smoothly, he handed Lina his phone and told her to call herself. Outside, in the car, he scrolled back up to her number and texted her: Want to come to a going away party?

When a person has lived for multiple years in a war zone, psychologists usually advise returning to careers that are thematically similar—fast-paced, chaotic, a little bit dangerous. You want to go hot to hot, rather than hot to cold. After three continuous years in the field, O'Dell wanted to return to the U.S. with Lina and start a new life. She was pregnant, and they planned to get married. But he worried that a safe, organized office job would destroy him. "People always ask me *why Baltimore?*" he says. You can find that answer on the news.

I would like a job overseeing scientific objectivity in a disorganized police agency in one of the most murder-prone cities in America, please, is not a usual career mission statement, but it worked for O'Dell. In 2013, while still overseas, he interviewed with the Baltimore Police Department over the phone. He flew back to the U.S. for a second interview, then took a train to visit family up in Vermont, where he promptly had another massive heart attack. This time, his new wife convinced him to let her drive him to a hospital, where he was admitted, and had emergency, rib-cracking, open heart surgery. The doctor informed him that he had had at least two previous heart attacks. Maybe more. *You shouldn't be alive*, the doctor said.

While O'Dell was still in the hospital, BPD offered him a position as a deputy director, overseeing the department's in-house laboratories. With Lina's help, he recovered enough for them to move to Baltimore with their daughter, renting a place while they looked for something to buy. By 2015, one of the police department's elite task forces, charged with getting guns off the streets, was under investigation by the DEA.* The riots that resulted from the death of Freddie Gray in police custody were all over the national news. That same year, there were 344 murders, 55 per 100,000 people—at the time, the highest per capita murder rate in the city's history. O'Dell wasn't happy about any of this. But when holding an umbrella under an unending fountain of bullshit,

---

* As of 2020, a state commission was still concluding a review of the actions of Baltimore's Gun Trace Task Force. Six former members had pleaded guilty in federal court, and two more had been convicted of racketeering conspiracy, racketeering, and robbery.

he was in his element. As far as he was concerned, his new job was perfect.

EVERY MORNING, O'DELL WAKES up at seven a.m. in his townhome halfway between Baltimore and Washington, DC. He puts on a dress shirt and tie, or a full suit, depending on what he's doing that day. People in the labs here can wear what they want (although that's not true everywhere), but O'Dell figures it's best for someone in his position to at least mirror the level of formality of the people he meets. Sometimes it's just a community group, but sometimes it's VIPs from outside the department; or his boss, the deputy commissioner.

O'Dell is at his desk by eight. What he does, mostly, is solve problems. Crime scene investigation at nearly every organization in the country is very much a team sport. By the time a person gets to O'Dell's level, a whole legion of other people is handling the nitty gritty decisions about where to look for DNA or which gun to investigate or whether two fingerprints match. A division head rides the leviathan at the very top, piloting it, ensuring that the entire enterprise is heading in the right direction financially, organizationally, and philosophically. What you want in a job like O'Dell's is a bit of a visionary, although it doesn't always work out that way.

When O'Dell arrived in 2013, he believed that Baltimore's crime lab was not oriented in the correct direction at all. It was run by a man O'Dell describes as "a bit of a mad scientist." He wasn't a bad guy; O'Dell just felt that the position required more of a people person. Unfortunately, forensics often leads to prime examples of the Peter Principle (in management theory, a person in an organization who is promoted high enough where they are no longer competent in their position) in action: the hard science skills that make excellent technicians and analysts don't always translate once you're at a policymaking level, having to convince commissioners and elected officials to trust you and provide you with resources. "Most of the job is managing relationships," O'Dell says. Employee to employee. Employee to lawyer. The whole department to political bodies, the sworn division, and the community.

In 2013, the sworn division and the lab were barely on speaking terms. Processes weren't streamlined, and the detectives felt like the scientists were talking down to them, force-feeding them jargon, not really helping with all their biochemical mumbo-jumbo. DellaRocco had had it. She was ready to leave if something didn't change. And then it did: when he had interviewed for the job back in Iraq, O'Dell had promised to smooth over the personality issues in the department. He got to work doing it.

O'Dell had always succeeded handily, but as literally every single person above him retired, quit, or was forced out over the next few years, he shot up in the department. He wrangled Baltimore's forensics operation from a buried departmental backwater to a division coequal with sworn officers, creating, in the process, a behemoth. Now, the Forensic Science and Evidence Services Division includes the in-house labs; the on-scene mobile unit; evidence control; research and records; and a burgeoning office that handles data from officers' body-worn cameras, which have become more common in law enforcement since the spate of police brutality cases that made headlines in the mid-2010s. To ensure that none of Baltimore's three divisions—the scientists, the patrol officers, and the detectives—could put their foot on the neck of the others, all three had to be equally powerful. O'Dell had to be a chief.

The social network LinkedIn is a powerful connector within the forensics community and—not surprisingly, given how many opportunities have come his way from that direction—O'Dell is wildly active on it. Not long after he started moving up in the Baltimore Police Department, he began writing posts that explored the job's philosophy and best practices. One post covered his strategy for Baltimore. "I don't know what everyone else plans to do, but I have been making changes and continue to do so," he wrote. "I am trying new things, I am trying some old things with new twists, but what I am NOT doing is doing the same thing and calling it something different."

Soon after O'Dell arrived, he pitched ideas to a *Shark Tank*–style innovation fund the City of Baltimore had in place, where public services could give proposals before a panel of local business owners who could vote to fund them. One of his ideas was to digitize the photography unit, saving $100,000 a year on photography supplies. He called that idea "Megapixel Madness," he says, because it was lunacy that a police department was still using film to document crime scenes in 2014. The panel agreed so strongly they told him they were going to give him the money while he was still in the room.

O'Dell continued looking for smarter ways to do things: A city master lease program that would allow the department to rent equipment for the drug lab and replace it before it got out-of-date. iPad apps that crime scene services could use to electronically document scenes, which O'Dell saw at an industry conference. Rana DellaRocco's probabilistic genotyping pitch.

Under O'Dell's direction, the ship righted itself so abruptly that even people outside the department noticed. The crime lab won a "Most Innovative Budget" award from the City of Baltimore for fiscal year 2018. ("Who would think you could be innovative in your budget?" O'Dell says.) The firearms unit made it into the top twenty NIBIN sites. O'Dell personally was named one of the 40 under 40 by the International Association of Chiefs of Police, an honor given to law enforcement professionals, including special investigators, managers, commissioners, chiefs, and captains from all over the world, who have gone beyond the call of duty. DellaRocco herself gave up the idea of abandoning Baltimore for someplace shinier. "The chief was the only reason I stayed at that time. Period," she says.

In 2018, O'Dell's daughter Bella, then five, was diagnosed with stage four neuroblastoma. It wrecked him. His wife spent every single night sleeping next to her at Johns Hopkins Hospital, and O'Dell eked out hours at the office whenever he could find them—the middle of the night, odd hours of the morning, any minute he wasn't traveling back and forth to Bella's room. The department was steadfastly supportive, once he got up the nerve to admit to them that he was having a personal crisis. But his original plan of steering the beast from six a.m. to six p.m. every single day was trashed.

Just three weeks ago, Johns Hopkins gave O'Dell's daughter the all clear, and she even got to ring a little bell and read a heart-wrenching statement about defeating the monster that had been inside her. Now that she's home, O'Dell has been putting in a respectable eight to four thirty at the department—a little less time than he used to. Circumstance has forced him to pay attention to what really matters. Still, he'll usually open his computer back up once he gets home and squeeze in a few last emails from his home office. Through the hardest challenge of his life, the work hasn't slowed at all. The other day he had to let someone go. Then some bonehead used a racist term for a person of Arabic descent in an open meeting and he'd had to deal with that. Over the weekend, there'd been seventeen shootings and three homicides. It never ends around here.

Today, though. Today is quiet. KT Jaeger, a cop-turned–firearms expert–turned lawyer, who, in addition to being the director of Baltimore's mobile unit, is also O'Dell's best friend from Iraq, stopped by to chat. From the hallway, you could hear the two of them laughing. Merry Christmas.

10

LOS ANGELES

The Hertzberg-Davis Forensic Science Center rises out of the dusty Los Angeles chaparral like a monolith, a peach-and-sea-green glass facade skirting the edge of California State University's Los Angeles campus. From the outside, it is impossible to tell whether the building is academic or administrative. Is it the campus president's office? A political science hall? The school of engineering?

The building's ordinary exterior, however, is a front. Inside, it is full of people investigating crimes perpetrated in the Los Angeles area, from north of the Angeles National Forest down to Long Beach on the coast, and west past Malibu. The inner sanctum of this building, behind locked and frosted glass doors, is home to the separate but conjoined crime labs for the Los Angeles Police Department and the Los Angeles County Sheriff's Department.

Lest it seem like Baltimore's approach to crime scene investigation is the only option out there, consider Los Angeles. Within the Hertzberg-Davis Center, the LAPD's crime lab operates in parallel to the LACSD's crime lab, touching, and in some cases sharing, the exorbitantly expensive equipment, but otherwise functioning in complete independence, side by side. The LAPD's side is home to the oldest crime lab in the country, ever since police reformer August Vollmer, having researched the work of European criminalists, opened it in 1923.

Crime scene science at the LAPD is separated into two subdivisions, the same as in Baltimore, only—surprise!—the subdivisions here are completely different. A division called "forensic science" handles field investigation, firearms, drugs, serology, and trace evidence, while a "technical investigation" division handles approaches that require less science and more expertise—fingerprints, photography, polygraphs (lie detector tests, which the Baltimore labs don't handle at all), and electronics.

Because it is a fundamentally *applied* science, forensics becomes exceptionally tailored to the crime environment it works to police. The Los Angeles area is especially prone to breeding clandestine meth and PCP labs, so the LAPD has trained a hazardous chemical team to investigate them. One of their biggest scourges lately are honey butane oil labs, where home chemists refine marijuana resin in apartments using violently flammable chemicals. When officers uncover such a scene, the hazardous chemical forensic unit attempts to establish which drugs were under production using which methods, while also not blowing up an entire city block.

Another special thing about Los Angeles: both the LAPD and the LACSD labs are connected to the oldest continually operating master's program in criminalistics in the country, at Cal State LA. And it's all because of O. J. Simpson.

The same way the advent of crime TV shows marked a fundamental shift in the public's conception of forensic science, a historian could split crime scene investigation into pre– and post–O. J. Simpson. The 1994 case was one of the first times national news paid any attention to the field, and most of the attention was bad. Compelling evidence, including the blossoming science of DNA, seemed aligned against former all-American running back O. J. Simpson, who stood accused of stabbing to death his ex-wife, Nicole Brown Simpson, and her friend, Ron Goldman, outside Nicole's condo.

Simpson's defense team accused the LAPD of not only

racism in their pursuit of evidence but also egregious failures of protocol. Hourly news chyrons blared accusations and then confessions of crime lab impropriety: DNA evidence had been packaged in plastic. Chain-of-custody had been broken. Items were unlogged. Fingerprints missed. Shame, shame, shame.

Mechanical engineer Lou Hartman and architect Ken Mohr watched the coverage metaphorically holding their fingers over their eyes. The two had worked together and separately designing labs for the pharmaceutical, manufacturing, and biotech industries, as well as for the FBI. Mohr felt that facilities could be as much to blame for scientific misfires as the people who worked in them. In some crime labs, people were working without the necessary equipment. Labs were understaffed and overloaded. How could a person perform meticulous analyses under those conditions?

"We felt like the crime lab was getting a bad rap," Mohr says of the Simpson coverage. "They could only do the best they could do with the information, the technology, and the facilities they had." Mohr compared the failure to what would happen in the aerospace industry if you were trying to design a spaceship to go to Mars with a penknife in a bathroom. Police departments all over the country were (and in a few cases still are) laboring under these conditions—trying to perform cutting-edge science with resources limited by city budgets and red tape.

Hartman and Mohr saw an opportunity. They rebranded themselves as a company called Crime Lab Design and partnered with Fields-Devereaux, a Los Angeles–area architecture firm now called Harley Ellis Devereaux, which was performing a statewide needs assessment for California, recommending that Southern California's forensics capabilities be brought in line with those of other sciences. As one of the partners of the architecture firm, they entered a design competition to envision Los Angeles's next crime lab and won. After nearly a decade of planning and fundraising, the building opened in 2007, placing the LAPD and LACSD crime labs in close enough proximity that they could share some expensive resources. It was located on the campus of Cal State LA, so that students could both learn from the pros and help push forensic science into the future. The building was the Hertzberg-Davis Center.

"LET ME BUY YOU a coffee," says Donald Johnson, one of three full-time faculty members at Cal State LA's criminalistics program. Wise and affable, Johnson's got a distinct Yoda vibe. He shuffles ahead of me into the center's wide, gleaming hallways, holding doors and dipping his white head deferentially. On the left lapel of his tweed jacket sits a tiny, gold-limned Sherlock Holmes pin.

Lately, Donald Johnson has to stop walking occasionally to go down on one knee to alleviate the stress on his back, which has given him trouble for months. But back when he worked for the LACSD in the 1990s, he was a bit of a daredevil, the type who would go to any length to test his own abilities. Case in point: He heard about a flying school in the Mojave Desert, so he started taking lessons with a retired navy captain. He was soon performing in aerobatic contests all over the country.

It took a while for the new, protocol-driven approach to forensic science to ramp up post–O. J., Johnson says, even out here. Now, the LACSD employs nearly three hundred people to provide forensic support to the sheriff's department, but back then, Johnson was on a forensic biology team of six. His job was crisis management, lab work, slamming out reports, and catching as many bad guys as possible as quickly as possible.

Back then, forensic biologists at the LACSD went out

to scenes to collect evidence. It's one of the reasons crime scene science is depicted that way on *CSI*. One of Johnson's colleagues, Elizabeth Devine, went on to become a long-time technical advisor and producer on the show. And their lives seem like they were pretty cinematic: a photo in the hallway of the Hertzberg-Davis Center shows an action shot of a much younger Johnson rappelling down the side of the Industry Hills Sheraton Hotel to collect evidence that could show whether a woman had jumped or was pushed to her death. "The sheriff gave this to us as kind of a recruitment poster," he says.

In the 1990s, Johnson worked one case that has become a thread that has run through his entire forensic career. The scene itself wasn't so unusual: a garage in which two men had worked on cars. One of the men had been found deceased, elsewhere, with a hole in his head, but detectives believed the garage might hold clues.

Johnson traveled out to the garage with a detective and a crime scene photographer, and together they collected what they could. There wasn't much: no bloody footprints, arterial splashes, sprays, or fingerprints. Just a few circular drops of dried blood on the floor, which Johnson sampled.

Back at the lab, Johnson confirmed that the blood belonged to the dead man. That was good news for the investigation, but it wouldn't prove anything. When detectives confronted the garage's owner, he insisted that the dead man had cut his finger while they were working on a car. It was an excuse that detectives saw all the time at LA County: *It's the dead guy's blood, sure, but I had nothing to do with it.*

When Johnson explored the garage floor, he'd noticed something else in the bloodstains, teeny tiny chunks of pink. They were barely visible, too small for him to identify with the naked eye. When he looked under a microscope, however, he saw neurons. The chunks were very clearly bits of brain.

Johnson's lopsided smile twitches up at one corner when he remembers this moment. Like most crime scene investigators, he is energized by the idea of catching someone in a lie. "He was convicted of murder," he says.

When California State University's master's program lured Johnson away from the LACSD in the early 2000s, the faculty asked him to give a colloquium. He talked about the brain case. Now that he would have time for research, he wanted to develop a science to catch criminals the same way he had the owner of the garage. Was there a smaller, more reliable version of those brain bits that could prove bloodstains came from a mortal injury?

It took Johnson almost his entire tenure at Cal State to solve this problem. First, there were technical issues—he wanted to use microRNA, a class of roughly two thousand regulatory molecules that appear in different combinations in the body's various tissues and organs—to determine whether dried bloodstains came from the heart or the lungs or the liver, tissues that shouldn't be outside a human body except in circumstances of death. But first he had to develop tests to detect the microRNA, and that required partnering with a biomedical company called Kiagen. And then, which microRNAs he should even look for. He had found, for example, one that was expressed in both lung tissue and blood, but that wouldn't work. If the test came back positive, he still wouldn't know if the blood came from a mortal injury or a papercut.

There were administrative problems, too. Both the LAPD and LACSD labs worked with human tissue, but as an academic, Johnson didn't have access to it for research purposes. The coroner's office wasn't much help either—they conduct their own research but couldn't just lend out samples without mountains of approvals and paperwork.

Finally, Johnson got his hands on a couple of rat carcasses, which his students, or in some cases a marksman, shot or stabbed in front of white poster board, collecting dried blood samples they later evaluated for different types of microRNA. Johnson published two academic papers on the results, in 2014 and 2017, establishing proof of his concept. The first paper showed that you could detect microRNA from the brain in gunshot wounds to the head, but not from gunshot wounds to the chest. The second showed that you could detect microRNA from the liver in stab wounds to the abdomen.

Much more work remains before Johnson's technique will be accepted by courts. It wouldn't be able to stand on its own in real cases unless it was independently verified by other labs, attempted with human samples, and tested under different environmental conditions to determine how stable the markers are. And still, a judge could challenge the technique, claiming it is insufficiently established.

Johnson's academic work illuminates a larger concept that's important to understand about crime scene investigation: It is a heavily applied science, a professional career riding on top of a continuously shifting scientific base. Treatments considered standard or acceptable change over time, the same way they do in medicine. Unlike medicine, there is no exhaustive series of Food and

Drug Administration tests designed to ensure the public's safety.

How do you know when a new forensic technique is ready for prime time? Thankfully, the law has weighed in. The first time, back in 1923, a man named James Alphonso Frye appealed his conviction for second-degree murder, claiming the court should have allowed evidence from a novel blood pressure–based lie detector test. The appeals court said *no*. In the now-famous opinion, the court admitted that "just when a scientific principle or discovery crosses the line between the experimental and demonstrable stages is difficult to define," but "the thing from which the deduction is made must be sufficiently established to have gained general acceptance in the particular field in which it belongs." Bummer for Frye: because the blood pressure test wasn't a generally accepted technique, the court upheld his conviction. But for everyone else, the Frye Standard became an idea that guided admissibility for almost a century.

Seventy years later, in 1993, the Supreme Court case *Daubert v. Merrell Dow Pharmaceuticals, Inc.* added some nuance to the Frye decision. Two children, Jason Daubert and Eric Schuller, had been born with birth defects, and their parents had sued Merrell Dow, claiming that a prescription anti-nausea drug the mothers had taken during pregnancy had caused the problems. When the parents showed up in court with evidence from their own experts that contradicted more relevant and established science, the Supreme Court was forced to weigh in on what constituted scientific expertise, and how a court could be expected to decide one way or another.

In the end, the Supreme Court decided that the Frye Standard was too stringent, vacated the lower court's ruling, and kicked the case back down. This time, they decided, the case would be adjudicated according to more lenient guidelines, which came to be known as the Daubert Standard: a court could consider multiple factors when deciding what evidence was allowed and what was not, including whether a theory or technique had been tested, peer reviewed, or published; what error rates were involved; whether there were existing standards for its use; and— back to the Frye idea—whether it was generally accepted by scientists in the appropriate field. The Daubert decision opened legal proceedings to newer scientific techniques, but ultimately, it came down to what the judge decreed: she would be the gatekeeper.

Crime scene scientists are, when it comes down to it,

archaeologists for living events. They use standard, universal tools to do their work. But when a complicated, nonstandard case crops up, they do what an archaeologist would do and develop, or find, a new tool that will answer any outstanding questions. Sometimes this has troublesome consequences: forensic scientists are only human, and faults in technique or theory that affect human lives may not become obvious for decades. The only solution is to work diligently, document meticulously, follow the scientific method, and always be ready to be wrong.

"Can I show you something?" Johnson says. We're sitting in a conference room in the Hertzberg-Davis Center, where posters of famous Los Angeles cases—the night stalker murders, the lonely hearts killer—decorate the walls. Johnson lopes off to his office, returning with a photocopy of his own blue script slanting across wide-ruled paper.

If I Could Have Three Wishes, the paper says. It is a photocopy of a third-grade writing assignment that Johnson's mother kept and sent to him when he was hired by the LACSD in 1989.

> *If I Could Have Three Wishes*
> *I would wish for*

> *A robot, just like the one in my book of*
>> The Runaway Robot.
> *A crime lab in my bedroom, police radio*
>> *also, doors that open on the roof so the*
>> *helicopter can come out.*
> *A helicopter, just like the one in the book of*
>> Tomorrow's Vehicles.

Farther down, Johnson says he wanted both the helicopter and the crime lab so he could "watch over the city, find out things, and get criminals."

To which most would say, *nice work.*

11

CSI

I put on an episode of *CSI*. And not one of the goofy ones where Gil Grissom snaps on his sunglasses and wings out a zinger like "and they call this safe sex" while the camera pans over to a guy strangled to death with a ligature made of condoms or something.

No. I put on longtime technical lead and producer Elizabeth Devine's favorite episode. It was the first one she wrote herself, based on one of the eight hundred or so cases she worked as a criminalist at the LACSD. Season 1, Episode 16: "Too Tough to Die." The episode fictionalizes the case of a real woman, Lois Haro, who was abducted from the parking lot of a Pasadena mall in 1988, robbed, raped, and murdered. In real life, Haro was left for dead in the dirt alongside an isolated road. She passed on the way to the hospital. In the show, she hangs on in a coma—a Jane Doe waiting in limbo between life and death. Devine made that change (and several others) on purpose. She wanted the episode to highlight legal loopholes that could hinder justice, leaving a crime scene investigator certain of what happened, but unable to do anything about it.

Criminalists talk a lot of well-deserved trash about *CSI*. The show has dramatically increased the number of applicants to forensic positions and forensic education programs, and those applicants are not always prepared to take on the actuality of the daily grind. The show has, arguably, altered the expectations of jurors, who enter courtrooms assuming the scientific analyses will be exhaustive and conclusive, and that every police department has the resources, and desire, to apply obscure techniques to even very simple cases.

In just this one episode, the actors employ a slate of tactics so thorough that, if a busy forensic unit applied them to every real case, they'd have a backlog so bloated it would be coming out the windows. On the show, the criminalists perform inter-views, consult on an autopsy, and reconstruct a shooting with a self-healing mannequin. At one point, Gil Grissom collects a scent sample and gives it to trained dogs to track down a suspect.*

---

* Incidentally, one of Gil Grissom's one-liners in this episode is simply stating Locard's principle outright: "Locard's principle," he says to one of the impressionable young bucks on the squad. "He took a piece of her away with him, and he left a piece of himself here. We get to find it."

I asked Chief O'Dell if he'd ever worked a crime scene with scent dogs. No, he said, as if I'd asked if he wore a hat made of cheese. What about bugs? Did he pick up bugs with tweezers? He'd only been involved in a couple of scenes that required insect knowledge, he said, but mostly because one of his core biology professors at UAB was a forensic entomologist, an insect expert.

Dull as it sounds, most of your standard crimes can be solved with a combination of photography, DNA evidence, serology, fingerprints, ballistics comparison, drug chemistry, and, lately, computer forensics, which is why these departments are standard across the country. There are all kinds of high-tech scientific subspecialties that could tell jurors more about how crimes occurred—really incredible stuff—but if a cash-strapped police department can do it easier and more cheaply using a typical technique, they're not going to bother with any of it. You don't have to plumb the depths of a case down to its last detail to solve it; you just have to solve it.

What else *could* crime scene investigators do? Bloodstain pattern analysis, for one thing. Donald Johnson teaches it in a modular soundstage in the Hertzberg-Davis Center with a mannequin and pigs' blood procured from a local slaughterhouse. Instructors splash the blood across the walls and floors, smear it over the mannequins' genitals, and drip it on dirty mattresses, so that students can learn concepts from actual scenes, including some Johnson worked himself.

Bloodstain pattern analysis (also known as blood spatter analysis, but under absolutely no circumstances blood "splatter" analysis) is very, very cool. Practitioners consider the size, shape, distribution, and location of stains at a crime scene to reconstruct the sequence of events that created them. It's physics in reverse: Blood is a liquid that behaves according to established principles. If it spurted out of an artery, it will leave a predictable pattern that will be different from the one left if it dripped off a pipe, sprayed out of a gunshot wound, or was smeared on the floor as a murderer dragged a body from place to place. Software such as HemoSpat can even help practitioners draw suspected lines and angles of impact, so CSIs trained in the subspecialty don't have to build them by hand with lasers or string.

The Baltimore Police Department has only used bloodstain pattern analysis to solve a crime once, O'Dell says, but most of the larger police departments have a person or three who are certified to do it just in case. Lately, the LAPD has been encouraging green analysts to pursue the training, so that they can point evidence collectors toward those stains most likely to supply revealing DNA.

One reason bloodstain pattern analysis hasn't been embraced more wholeheartedly by police agencies is that it exists in an epistemological gray area: it involves a profound amount of math, but there is a worrying amount of subjectivity to the interpretation. "I'm on the fence about it," DellaRocco says. "It's one of those things where, if this is the only bit of evidence that we have, or it's a last-ditch effort, then Steve *might* consult on it." (Among Chief O'Dell's endless catalog of capabilities is a lapsed certification—but standing expertise—in bloodstain pattern analysis.)

But even O'Dell isn't an evangelist for the technique: "Bloodstains tell you less about who did it than about where they were standing when they might have done it," he says. "Its most powerful purpose is if you come in and say, *I wasn't there*, and I can say, *these are impact spatters on your clothes; you had to have been there*." The problem, O'Dell says, is that then a criminal could reply, *Okay, I was there, but I didn't do it*. It's another version of the alibi Donald Johnson ran into in LA County: murderers, as it turns out, really don't like to admit to murders.

What else have you seen on TV that crime scene investigators do in real life? Trace evidence analysis, the chemical or physical comparison of shoe prints, tire tracks, carpet or clothing fibers, paint swatches, accelerants, and other miscellany, is real. Most departments maintain labs or experts to perform it, often to generate leads when more definitive evidence isn't available. Baltimore employs just one person to investigate trace evidence. He handles about sixty (mostly arson-related) cases a year. Because his work requires the same GC-MS machines the drug lab uses, he shares their equipment.

Forensic anthropologists, sometimes called "buried body" or bone experts, can get called in from medical examiners' offices and local universities to examine or dig up bones. The conclusions these experts can draw from partial skeletons found with few identifying possessions can be uncanny. In her fascinating and at times horrifying 2004 autobiography *Teasing Secrets from the Dead*, forensic anthropologist Emily Craig recounts how she categorized and separated the remains of victims in the Branch Davidian Compound in Waco, Texas; the Oklahoma City bombing; and the terrorist attacks on the World Trade Center from little more than charred fragments.

Another specialty you may see in lists of crime lab

capabilities are questioned documents labs. (Again, Baltimore employs just one person for this. He has a light enough caseload that he moonlights as a drug chemist.) The purview of QD is to determine through the analysis of inks, papers, printing characteristics, handwriting, and signatures whether important contracts, receipts, notes, or other papers have been forged or are otherwise not what they seem. QD labs are not as common as they once were (you can thank computers for that), but most large jurisdictions retain the expertise just in case. The master of this specialty, believe it or not, is the U.S. Secret Service, which began as an agency to fight money counterfeiting, and now maintains a forensic unit with the largest ink library in the world (containing more than twelve thousand samples) and a computerized handwriting database called FISH, the Forensic Information System for Handwriting.

I've barely mentioned digital forensics in this book because it is an area of expertise that could support its own book. Historically, analysis of computers has been used to bring down child pornographers, fraud rings, and stalkers (as well as murderers, such as the infamous BTK killer, who have the poor foresight to communicate with police by mailing them floppy disks), but in recent years the ubiquity of personal devices has made digital evidence as useful as anything that can be collected in the physical world. Digital forensics experts collect and analyze evidence from hard drives, smartphones, networks, and the cloud, searching for deleted files, banking transactions, Google searches, text messages, or posts on message boards, connections to other criminals, dark web purchases, or anything else suspicious. While the Bureau of Labor Statistics doesn't maintain a separate accounting of computer forensics careers from the remainder of the forensic field, information security analyst jobs are in great demand and only growing. Jobs in that field are expected to increase by 31 percent by 2029, and median pay clocks in at an impressive $99,730 a year.

Then there's the really niche stuff. UK-based forensic ecologist and botanist Patricia Wiltshire (author of the 2019 autobiography *The Nature of Life and Death*) has solved hundreds of otherwise uncrackable forensic puzzles using pollen, fungal spores, plants, trees, and dirt. Jessica Metcalf, a professor at Colorado State University, is developing a death clock based on the sequence of microbial communities that bloom in a body postmortem. Andrea Zaferes, a death investigator in Dutchess County, New York, specializes in "homicidal drowning," and has cataloged, in detail, all the ways water currents can drag a body from a dumping site. "Believe it or not, there are forensic locksmiths," Rana DellaRocco says. Baltimore had to find one a year ago when they found a key fob to a car that had been lit on fire.

If you were writing a TV show, incorporating esoteric techniques such as these would stoke interest across a season, preventing the episodes from getting repetitive. But for most forensic analysts? The episodes get repetitive. Those who work full-time in crime labs plug along, day after day, doing the real, prosaic work. Experts who handle the wild, crazy stuff usually maintain their own private practices, do their specialty analyses on the side of full-time lab jobs, or work full- or part-time in academia, consulting on cases only when called.

Am I saying nothing about *CSI* is realistic? Not at all. Devine worked hard to make the show reflect her own experience as much as she could under Hollywood's crushing directive to create drama.

The long hours are real. Intradepartmental personality clashes are real. The machines the actors beep and boop on the show are based on those that Devine used at the LA County Sheriff's Department in the 1980s and 1990s. She had fights, she says, with set designers who wanted to draw chalk lines around bodies (literally no one does this). But the *most* accurate moment in Season 1, Episode 16 is when actress Jorja Fox, standing in for Elizabeth Devine, cries in a hospital hallway.

I hope it is clear by now that crime scene investigation is a career that places incredible demands on the people who practice it. It is a science job, sure, but one with some of the emotional demands of working in law enforcement or health care. Although they are less likely to encounter a crime in progress, CSIs who attend scenes see violent death more frequently than the average police officer does, and when they do, they spend more time in close proximity to it. They may meet friends or relatives of victims at the scene and hear their harrowing stories. In CSIs who don't manage stress effectively, the cumulative impact can lead to burn-out, compassion fatigue, post-traumatic stress, excessive drinking, and even divorce.

In "Too Tough to Die," Jorja Fox's hard-charging crimi-nalist Sara Sidle is well on her way to some of these prob-lems. Because she is a television character, we don't know whether Sidle started out with higher ratings of death anxi-ety than the average population, or had lower emotional intelligence scores, or employed mostly avoidance-based behavioral and cognitive coping tactics, all of which are associated with increased levels of stress in CSIs. But she's certainly very type A, a personality style that you'd want to watch carefully in a profession like this. (Rana DellaRocco appears to be doing just fine.)

Sidle also employs few stress-management practices. At least in this early episode, she's not shown doing yoga or meditating or talking to a therapist or friends. She doesn't seem to have a sense of humor; she doesn't golf or crochet or collect old records. Instead, she searches through missing persons logs all night trying to identify her Jane Doe. She holds on to the victim's locket, hoping to give it to someone who loves and misses her. She gets emotionally involved in the case. And at the end of the episode, when she learns that the assailant won't be appropriately punished because of an age-related technicality, she breaks down in a hospital hallway. Not a lot of people want to talk about that, but it happens.

"I'll be brutally honest about it," says Emma Sentz.

Sentz is yet another crime scene investigator, from yet another department who has had yet another completely different career path. A former army police sergeant who now works at the only private crime scene investigations firm in the country, Laura Pettler & Associates, down in Monroe, North Carolina, Sentz used to supervise the crime scene unit in Frederick, Maryland, an operation about fifty miles west of Baltimore that is much smaller, and, by extension, much more intimate.

Frederick wasn't nearly as busy as Baltimore. Sentz worked on a team of just three people that sent swabs and fingerprint lifts out to state labs for processing. The crime scene team didn't have to go from scene to scene the way the crime laboratory technicians in Baltimore do, which made it harder to distance themselves from those crimes that were particularly gruesome.

No matter how even-keeled you are, if you attend crime scenes, one of them will eventually get to you, and which one it is may be a surprise. You would expect to be emotionally disturbed by the murder of a child, for example, but might find yourself breaking down over a beaten dog or a suicide or some other ostensibly lesser crime. The scene that broke through Elizabeth Devine's defenses involved a murdered woman who looked just like her grandmother. "I left my notebook at the scene. I had to go back and get it, I mean I was a wreck," she says.

Sentz had the worst time when the victims were still alive

and could tell her what they'd suffered. Once, she worked three child rapes in a two-week period, two at the hands of their fathers. Faith got her through it, she says. Faith, and righteous anger. She met every single one of those little girls, processed their bodies. "One girl drew us a map to where [the man's] semen stains would be," she says of the last of the three.

In that case, the girl's younger sister wasn't even two years old. Semen stained parts of the nursery. Downstairs from where Sentz was processing the scene, the mother was defending her husband. The girl lies, the mother was saying. She's always telling stories to get attention.

Sentz would have done this anyway, she says, but she annihilated that house looking for evidence. She ripped up the carpet, took a saw to the wall. "Call your daughter a liar," she thought to herself. "I just found your husband's semen next to your baby's crib."

When she got home from that one, she called her mom because she wasn't sure she could say what she needed to say to her father. She cried. And then the next day she went back to work.

There aren't many people out there who can divorce themselves from their emotions enough to walk into hell and process it into cold, streamlined logic. Sentz, and the other people in this book, are a few of them. In Sentz's case, she believes her ability to do her job is a god-given gift. "If I *can* do this, then I have to," she says. Most people would run screaming in the other direction, and then who would be left to serve those poor little girls?

It may have been God or genes or a happy confluence of internal fortitudes that gave Sentz the ability to do this work. It doesn't matter. Lucky for us, there are thousands more like her out there, acting in the place of broken surveillance cameras, peering beneath the facades of liars, defending the public through science and logic. Since shows like *CSI* began to show us how incredible this job is, the number of people willing to perform it has grown, year after year, into an inexhaustible phalanx. Every time any of its thousands of members heads out to a crime scene and finds what she's looking for, another criminal loses his ability to hurt the rest of us. And every time a young person puts on an episode of *CSI* and falls under its spell, we get another shield.

ACKNOWLEDGMENTS

This book would not have even begun if it weren't for Hayden B. Baldwin at International Crime Scene Investigators Association, who directed me to Glen Calhoun at the International Association for Identification, who invited me out to the IAI's annual conference, sight unseen. Of course, after that it wouldn't have gone anywhere without the massive trust placed in me by Baltimore Police Crime Lab chief Steven O'Dell, who was candid with my questions, excited about the project, and willing to let me bother his entire department repeatedly and at length.

I owe a massive debt to Michael Kessler, Research Project Manager at the National Forensic Science Technology Center and Instructor at the International Forensic Research Institute, who sent me research papers and reading recommendations, answered my endless questions with an unfathomable degree of patience, and read several chapters.

Douglas Starr, professor of journalism at Boston University and science writer extraordinaire, provided helpful guidance on reporting the history of criminalistics. Many thanks to Buffy Miller at the LAPD for an overview of the way they do things out west, Michael Lee at the Michigan State Police Department for an overview of the way they do things up north, and Ross Gardner, formerly of the United States Army Criminal Investigation Command and the Lake City, Georgia, police, and currently of Bevel, Gardner & Associates consulting group, for an overview of the way they do things down south. Thank you to Everett Baxter Jr., who helped me wrap my head around how CSI is taught. Thank you to Mark Listewnik, senior editor at CRC Press, for introducing me to a number of these people.

Michael Lawson, probabilistic genotyping maven at the Baltimore Police Department, went over my DNA science with a molecularly fine-toothed comb, as did Greg Hampikian at Boise State University. Former *CSI* producer Elizabeth Devine spent one of the most entertaining hours I've ever experienced regaling me with stories from her days in the field and, later, in Hollywood. Kendall (KT) Jaeger and Cinese Caldwell, the heads of Baltimore's on-scene crime unit, despite appearing only briefly in this book, are two of the most helpful and forthcoming people at the Baltimore Police Department. They researched the answers to farragoes of questions and provided me with statistics to an astounding degree of depth. I can't say enough about how hardworking, kind, and generous everyone I met down in Baltimore was. Thank you all.

Finally, I'd like to thank my husband, Alexander George, for unending patience, support, and always knowing when I could use a beer or a coffee or both.

APPENDIX I
WILDLY DIFFERENT DIRECTIONS

A background in hard science and forensics can lead a person toward dozens of different exciting careers, like pushing through a bottleneck into a wonderland. A marvelous thing about this industry is that it encompasses any science that might be useful for identifying victims and finding bad guys. If you're into human anatomy, there will be something you can do to help. Same if you're into computers, chemicals, animals, dentistry, or even the mail. If you think solving crime with science is for you, but aren't sure you want to work for a state lab or a police department, here are a few other areas in the wide world of forensics worth checking out.

FORENSIC ANTHROPOLOGY: UNIVERSITY OF
TENNESSEE FORENSIC ANTHROPOLOGY CENTER

https://fac.utk.edu/

Forensic anthropologists are the experts a police department would call for help removing, identifying, and analyzing bones found at a possible crime scene. There are now academic programs in the science at many large universities, but the program at the University of Tennessee, which began in 1987, has trained some of the foremost forensic anthropologists in the country, including at the FBI. UT's program was also the first to operate an outdoor decomposition research facility, nicknamed "the body farm," where donated human remains are allowed to decompose under natural circumstances to provide control data for scientists. There are now at least a half dozen of these, including at Texas State University, Sam Houston State University (also in Texas), Western Carolina University, Colorado Mesa University, and Southern Illinois University.

VETERINARY FORENSICS:
ASPCA ANIMAL FORENSIC SCIENCES

https://www.aspca.org/animal-rescue/forensic-investigations

If you've ever seen one of those Sarah McLachlan ASPCA commercials, you'll know that not all crimes involve humans. If you'd like to stand up for the defenseless animals who are sometimes victims of violence or cruelty, you may be interested in veterinary forensics. The American Society for the Prevention of Cruelty to Animals (ASPCA)'s professional forensic services team employs evidence collection, DNA analysis, necropsies (animal autopsies), and other techniques to bust puppy mills and animal-fighting rings. The organization has a partnership with the University of Florida to offer a special program in the field (https://forensics.med.ufl.edu/).

MAIL CRIME: UNITED STATES POSTAL INSPECTION SERVICE'S NATIONAL FORENSIC LABORATORY

https://www.uspis.gov

So many crimes are perpetrated through the postal system that the USPS has operated its own bureau of investigation to investigate mail-based fraud, Ponzi schemes, bombings, child exploitation, and drug crimes since roughly 1775. This agency, the Postal Inspection Service, includes an accredited forensics lab in Dulles, Washington, where scientists apply physical, chemical, and digital skills to investigate explosives, toolmarks, unknown chemicals, questioned documents, fibers, and pretty much anything else you can think of. They even have their own *CSI*-style television show, called *The Inspectors*.

DIGITAL FORENSICS: THE NATIONAL COMPUTER
FORENSICS INSTITUTE (NCFI)

https://www.ncfi.usss.gov

Scores of universities offer degrees in computer forensics, and ethical hacking or cybersecurity work is another good way in. But if you're already a law enforcement officer, a judge, or a prosecutor and you want to tack computer expertise on to your qualifications while learning from the big dogs, the NCFI is a good option. The organization is a partnership between the Secret Service, the Department of Homeland Security, and the State of Alabama where it is located, and offers courses focusing on digital currency, social networking, mobile devices, and malware analysis, among other topics, in the hopes of preventing cybercrimes that endanger U.S. financial and civil infrastructure.

ARSON INVESTIGATION: ATF FIRE RESEARCH
LABORATORY

atf.gov/laboratories/fire-research-laboratory

While other fire research laboratories might focus on preventing or containing forest fires, or developing flame-resistant building materials, the one run by the Bureau of Alcohol, Tobacco, Firearms, and Explosives specifically supports investigations into arson, fire spread, and fire starts. They do this by, basically, lighting all sorts of things on fire. Their large burn room is so huge, at fifteen thousand square feet, with a fifty-foot roof, it can re-create fires on a two-story house.

BOMB ANALYSIS: FBI TERRORIST EXPLOSIVE DEVICE ANALYTICAL CENTER (TEDAC)

https://www.fbi.gov/services/laboratory/tedac

Similar to a firearms analysis lab, but focusing on improvised explosive devices, TEDAC examines explosives found both within and outside the United States, investigating them for DNA, fingerprints, toolmarks, and signature chemicals or bomb-building styles that might lead authorities to a known maker. Various units also perform controlled explosions, safety assessments, and support at bombing scenes.

MEDICAL AND MORTUARY SERVICES: THE NATIONAL DISASTER MEDICAL SYSTEM (NDMS) AND DISASTER MORTUARY OPERATIONAL RESPONSE TEAMS (DMORTs)

https://www.phe.gov/Preparedness/responders/ndms/Pages/default.aspx

It's not pleasant to think about, but when natural or man-made disasters such as earthquakes, large-scale bombings, or other mass-casualty events occur, someone has to sort through and identify the bodies of those who succumbed. Often, DMORTs, deployable forces made up of funeral directors, medical examiners, pathologists, forensic anthropologists, fingerprint specialists, forensic dentists, X-ray technicians, and dental assistants, assist local authorities in getting the work done.

CHEMICAL WARFARE FORENSICS: THE UN-OPCW
JOINT INVESTIGATIVE MECHANISM (JIM)

https://www.opcw.org/

Ever wonder how international watchdog organizations know when a country is breaking international conventions on chemical weapons? Mostly through this group, the investigational arm of the United Nations Security Council and the Organization for the Prohibition of Chemical Weapons. Headquartered in The Netherlands, this group of chemistry experts can be deployed whenever a dictator or rogue warlord is suspected of using banned chemical techniques against their enemies.

APPENDIX II
FURTHER READING

THE SERIOUS STUFF

Baxter Jr., Everett. *Complete Crime Scene Investigation Handbook.* Boca Raton, FL: CRC Press, 2015.

This is the book that the pros down in Baltimore learn from, a floor-to-ceiling overview of practical criminalistics by Oklahoma-based instructor Everett Baxter Jr. You can purchase it with a companion lab exercise workbook, which new CSIs use for hands-on classes, but which a diligent independent studier could use at home to get a leg up on her competition.

Camarillo, Dana L., ed. *Hertzberg-Davis Forensic Science Center.* http://file.lacounty.gov/SDSInter/lasd/144942_Hertzberg -Davis.pdf.

This detailed history of building Los Angeles's Hertzberg-Davis Center will mostly interest public architecture buffs (those exist, right?), but the real gems in this e-book created for the unveiling of the new facility are the descriptions of the layout and working areas, the early days of crime scene investigation at the LAPD and LACSD, and the history of police science education at Cal State LA. Los Angeles is the seat of modern crime scene investigation in the United States, and it's worth learning how that came to be.

Cobain, Ian. "Killer Breakthrough: The Day DNA Evidence First Nailed a Murderer." *The Guardian*. (June 7, 2016) https://www.theguardian.com/uk-news/2016/jun/07/killer-dna-evidence-genetic-profiling-criminal-investigation.

I gleaned much of the history of Alec Jeffreys's discovery of DNA fingerprinting from videos and materials provided by the University of Leicester, but several details, particularly of the Dawn Ashworth and Lynda Mann case, came from this thirty-year retrospective by British journalist Ian Cobain. It reads like a provincial UK crime thriller, with talk of pubs and pints and charming towns beset by a maniac.

Gardner, Ross M., and Donna R. Krouskup. *Practical Crime Scene Processing and Investigation*. Boca Raton, FL: CRC Press, 2018.

The CRC Press is the main game in town when it comes to textbooks on forensic sciences. The titles on their website are so specific you can find almost anything you're looking to learn, including *Forensic Gait Analysis*; *Cybercrime Investigations*; and 388 pages on *Asphyxiation, Suffocation, and Neck Pressure Deaths* (yikes). This book, by former military investigator and current crime scene reconstruction consultant Ross Gardner, is another favorite for training new CSIs.

Gross, Hans. *Criminal Investigation: A Practical Handbook for Magistrates, Police Officers and Lawyers*. London: Forgotten Books, 2018.

The original nineteenth-century field guide to criminalistics is packed with surprisingly readable case studies and is as fascinating as ever. Gross arrives at the conclusions that have guided the field of criminalistics for more than a century, while also recounting the travails of "peasants," "highwaymen," "gipsies," "devils," and other anachronisms.

Hatcher, Julian S. *Hatcher's Notebook*. Mechanicsburg, PA: Stackpole Books, 1962.

Julian Hatcher was chief of the U.S. Army Ordnance Department's small arms division, technical editor of *The American Rifleman*, and director of the National Rifle Association for twenty-four years. Few people on Earth know more than he did about firearms, which is why the book he wrote to fill a hole in public knowledge on the subject remains as useful as it was when it was first published, in 1947.

Fisher, Barry A. J. and David R. Fisher. *Techniques of Crime Scene Investigation*. Boca Raton, FL: CRC Press, 2012.

This is an old-school, classic textbook featuring compelling case studies, detailed pictures, and reading comprehension questions at the ends of chapters. It is comprehensive and reflects the sciences you're likely to actually encounter in a real modern police department. You will come away from it feeling like you've taken an intro-level college course in crime scene investigation. Beware of the photos. Some are exceptionally graphic.

Kelty, Sally F., Roberta Julian, and James Robertson. "*Professionalism in Crime Scene Examination: The Seven Key Attributes of Top Crime Scene Examiners.*" *Forensic Science Policy & Management* 2, no. 4 (November, 2011): 175–186.

Although this research was conducted in Australia on CSEs, or "crime scene examiners," its findings apply to anyone doing this work (and probably people in lots of other careers as well). The researchers interviewed seventy-four people working in police departments and forensics agencies with the aim of establishing what traits an ideal crime scene investigator should have. They determined that, among other things, a great CSI should be a lateral thinker, experienced in highly charged situations, who has high credibility, a positive worldview, and doesn't whine.

King, William, William Wells, Charles Katz, Edward Maguire, and James Frank. *Opening the Black Box of NIBIN: A Descriptive Process and Outcome Evaluation of the Use of NIBIN and Its Effects on Criminal Investigations, Final Report.* (U.S. Department of Justice, 2013) www.ncjrs.gov/pdffiles1/nij/grants/243875.pdf.

As a rule, Department of Justice reports aren't particularly compelling reading, except for this one: a deep look inside the function and dysfunction of the National

Integrated Ballistic Information Network that includes a thorough background on the practice of firearms analysis, as well as some unexpected wit.

Kline, Michael. "CSI: St. Valentine's Day Massacre" *American Society of Arms Collectors Bulletin* 102 (Fall, 2010): 11–20. https://americansocietyofarmscollectors.org/wp-content/uploads/2019/06/2010-B102-CSI-St-Valentine-s-Day-Massacre.pdf.

This article based on a presentation to the American Society of Arms Collectors, a group of historians and arms aficionados who collect and study scholarly literature about guns and armor, includes an in-depth history of the St. Valentine's Day Massacre and Calvin Goddard's role in solving it. The coolest part is the photos—images of the gun room at the laboratory at Northwestern University, cartridge case comparisons, an early comparison microscope, and lots and lots of tommy guns.

Locard, Edmond. "The Analysis of Dust Traces. Part I." *The American Journal of Police Science* 1, no. 3 (May–June 1930): 276–298, https://www.jstor.org/stable/1147154.

Although not as useful now that few people work as "gun cotton workers" or "indigotiers," this article from

1930 explaining how to catch a criminal using dust is fascinating just for a look into the mind of Edmond Locard. The man was nothing if not thorough, and he really does sound like Sherlock Holmes.

McRoberts, Alan, ed., *The Fingerprint Sourcebook*. Washington, DC: U.S. Department of Justice Office of Justice Programs, 2012, https://www.ncjrs.gov/pdffiles1/nij/225320.pdf.

An absolutely depthless guide to fingerprints and their analysis, starting with the ancient Chinese use of hand-prints as identification and including the anatomy and development of friction ridge skin, background on AFIS, and even cognitive distortions that can occur during print comparison. Absolutely everything you have ever wondered about fingerprints is in here, down to the "relative abun-dance of amino acids in sweat." (It's mostly serine.)

Muehlberger, C. W. "Col. Calvin Hooker Goddard 1891–1955." *Journal of Criminal Law and Crimonology* 46, no. 1 (1955): 103, https://scholarlycommons.law.northwestern.edu/cgi /viewcontent.cgi?article=4351&context=jclc.

A brief (it's just two pages) but fascinating biography of Calvin Goddard, the godfather of firearms examination in the United States. It explains Goddard's highly impressive career arc, from the Army Medical Corps to the development of the dual microscope to serving as the managing editor of the *American Journal of Police Science.*

THE FUN STUFF

Craig, Emily. *Teasing Secrets from the Dead*. New York: Random House, 2004.

Although Emily Craig's memoir covers forensic anthropology more than crime scene investigation, it provides an intimate, firsthand look at how police and scientists work together as teams to process crimes so big you've seen them on the national news. It's also delightfully gross.

Doyle, Arthur Conan. *Sherlock Holmes: A Study in Scarlet.* (Project Gutenberg, 2008), https://www.gutenberg.org/files /244/244-h/244-h.htm.

All of Sir Arthur Conan Doyle's Sherlock Holmes stories are inspiring to budding crime scene investigators, but this one is the very first appearance of the fictional detective, published at the very beginning of the criminalistics craze in Europe. It is also the first time a magnifying glass was introduced to the public as an investigative tool.

Grisham, John. *The Innocent Man*. New York: Bennington Press, 2006.

The author of *The Firm* and *The Pelican Brief*'s first nonfiction book focuses on the miscarriage of justice in the tiny town of Ada, Oklahoma. It's overflowing with the kinds of mistakes crime scene investigators must constantly beware of: most important, assuming you know who's guilty and who isn't.

McDermid, Val. *Forensics: What Bugs, Burns, Prints, DNA, and More Tell Us About Crime*. New York: Grove Press, 2014.

Scottish crime writer Val McDermid did so much research on forensics while writing her best-selling suspense novels that she decided to put it all together in a nonfiction book on real crime solvers. This one ranges wildly through the field, covering anthropology, facial recognition, pathology, toxicology, and fire scene re-creation, in addition to the usual suspects.

Neff, James. *The Wrong Man: The Final Verdict on the Dr. Sam Sheppard Murder Case*. New York: Open Road Media, 2015.

Widely considered the inspiration for the 1993 hit movie *The Fugitive*, the Sam Sheppard murder case captivated the country when it hit newspapers in 1954. Sheppard, an attractive doctor, was accused of bludgeoning his pregnant wife to death, and his defense team had a hell of a time trying to convince a jury otherwise, at least until a very famous blood spatter analysis expert got involved.

Starr, Douglas. *The Killer of Little Shepherds*. New York: Random House, 2010.

A nonfiction book so deeply researched and compellingly written it reads like fiction, this one tells the story of the European "ripper" you've never heard of, France's Joseph Vacher, and the herculean efforts French scientists undertook to bring him down.

Wiltshire, Patricia. *The Nature of Life and Death*. New York: Penguin Random House, 2019.

Welsh scientist Patricia Wiltshire pretty much invented the field of forensic ecology, which is why most

of us have never heard of it. In her combination memoir and field guide, she writes about removing grains of
pollen from dead people's nasal cavities, using spores
to counter a rapist's claim that he had never been to
the scene of the crime, and other wizard-like activities.

ABOUT THE AUTHOR

Jacqueline Detwiler-George is the former articles editor of *Popular Mechanics* magazine and former host of the *Most Useful Podcast Ever*. Her reporting on cancer research appeared in *The Best American Science and Nature Writing*. She lives in Pennsylvania with her husband and an absurd number of plants.